THE SELF-MADE MAN IN AMERICA

THE SELF-MADE MAN IN AMERICA

THE MYTH OF RAGS TO RICHES

By IRVIN G. WYLLIE

THE FREE PRESS, *New York*
COLLIER-MACMILLAN LIMITED, *London*

Printed in the United States of America

Collier-Macmillan Canada, Ltd., Toronto, Ontario

Library of Congress Catalog Card Number: 54-10602

FIRST FREE PRESS PAPERBACK EDITION 1966

To my parents,

GORDON *and* ANNA WYLLIE

ACKNOWLEDGMENTS

THE boast of the self-made man that he owes nothing to others, that his accomplishments are his own, is not only ungenerous but largely untrue. In academic circles such claims are rare. Here the usual practice is to acknowledge scholarly debts, to advertise the contribution of the larger academic community to the creative work of the individual. Having herein derogated the self-made man's overweening sense of his own importance, I welcome the opportunity to honor this wise academic custom.

In the footnotes and essay on sources I acknowledge my indebtedness to men I have never met except through the printed page, men who, I gladly admit, thought my thoughts before me, and supplied many of the insights which I now claim as my own.

I owe my greatest debt to Merle E. Curti, Frederick Jackson Turner Professor of History at the University of Wisconsin, who aroused my first interest in the history of ideas and suggested this study of the rags-to-riches theme. His technical contributions to the project are too many to enumerate here. Important as they have been, they appear insignificant in relation to the encouragement and inspiration which he offered.

Professor Clifton C. Edom of the University of Missouri

School of Journalism called my attention to the Charles Dana Gibson drawings which have been reproduced herein with the gracious permission of Mrs. Charles Dana Gibson and her son, Langhorne Gibson.

Professor Fred Harvey Harrington of the Department of History of the University of Wisconsin ran his critical eye over an original draft of the manuscript, and made many suggestions for its improvement. I especially appreciate his counsel in behalf of simplicity, brevity, and directness. Dr. Roger W. Shugg, former director of the Rutgers University Press, suggested ways and means of rounding out the study.

Since I found my principal sources in Washington, I owe a special word of thanks to Dr. Wesley M. Gewehr of the Department of History of the University of Maryland, who favored me with a teaching schedule which enabled me to spend considerable time at the Congressional Library.

I also wish to express appreciation to Dr. James N. Primm, Assistant Director of the Western Historical Manuscripts Collection at the University of Missouri, for permitting me to exploit his staff. Mrs. Jane Peters typed the manuscript without adequate reward.

CONTENTS

THE SELF-MADE MAN IN AMERICA

THE AMBITION to succeed may be and always ought to be a laudable one. It is the ambition of every parent for his child. It is emphatically an American ambition; at once the national vice and the national virtue. It is the mainspring of activity; the driving wheel of industry; the spur to intellectual and moral progress. It gives the individual energy; the nation push. It makes the difference between a people that are a stream and a people that are a pool; between America and China. It makes us at once active and restless; industrious and overworked; generous and greedy. When it is great, it is a virtue; when it is petty, it is a vice.

—*Lyman Abbott*

Prologue

MEN WHO SEARCH for meaning in history know that it is difficult to divine the central tendency of an age or discover the ruling spirit of a people. Tendencies and spirits are as varied as men themselves, and the records which embody them are confused, faulty, and fragmentary. Occasionally, however, the record is very clear. Thirty years ago a perceptive American writer, Claude C. Washburn, suggested that the record of the American people would eventually be found in the ephemeral books and magazines preserved in the Library of Congress. He also predicted that these volumes would reveal that the principal American aspiration could be expressed by the single word Success. Indeed the gospel of success has been a noisy one through all our history, and thousands of evangelists have been enlisted in its service. The pulpit, the platform, and the press have overflowed with its catchwords, its aphorisms, and its instances. Across the land from Benjamin Franklin's day to our own, young men have sought direction and inspiration in its glittering lore.

But what is success? Americans have defined it in various ways. Politicians equate it with power, publicists with fame. Teachers and moralists rate themselves successful when they have influenced the minds and characters of others. Men of creative instinct strive for self-realization. Humanitarians identify success with service, reformers with the alteration of the social order. To the devout, success is salvation, and to thousands of plain people it is nothing more than contentment and a sense of happiness. Each of these definitions embodies worthy ideals, and all have their champions. But no one of these concepts enjoys such universal favor in America as that which equates success with making money. "Every one knows that success with the great masses spells money," said John C. Van Dyke in 1908 in his book *The Money God*. "It is money that the new generation expects to win, and it is money that the parents want them to win. The boy will make it, and the girl, if she is not a goose, will marry it. They will get it in one way or another."

Strangers to our shores have often commented on this our ruling passion—sometimes with distaste, occasionally with appreciation, always with wonder. In the 1830s that friendly critic of democracy, Alexis de Tocqueville, asserted that he knew of no other country where the love of money had a stronger hold on the affections of the people, or where wealth circulated so rapidly from generation to generation. Some years later the Englishman James Bryce reported that the most remarkable phenomenon of the preceding half century had been the rise of the American millionaire, a man whose triumphs nourished ambition, emulation, and envy. "The pursuit of wealth is nowhere so eager as in America," he observed, "the opportunities for acquiring it are nowhere so numerous." To Europeans our possessions were our principal glory, and worship of them, our principal fault. No American characteristic excited so much unfavorable comment as devotion to the dollar. Even today our boasting about material possessions tends to isolate us from other less fortunate peoples. In 1949, when the Common Council for American Unity sponsored a study of European beliefs regarding the United States, investigators discovered that Europeans still cling to the idea that Americans are too materialistic. This conviction breeds suspicions which stand in the way of better foreign understanding of the United States.

Europeans who share these misgivings assume that Americans value money for its own sake, that their interests do not extend beyond gold. Such assumptions have some basis in fact. Greedy men have often sacrificed virtue and justice upon the altar of Mammon, and valued lucre above learning, or religion, or love of country. It is a mistake, however, to deduce the motives of an entire people from the careers of a few representatives, for though some Americans look upon wealth as an end in itself, and sacrifice everything to its acquisition, many more view it only as an instrumentality. The view of the majority squares with that central precept of the folklore of success which says that money has no value except in relation to its uses. Even when foreign critics acknowledge the principle of utility they complain that we devote our substance to material ends. Who can deny it? We have used money to promote physical progress, but the crucial fact is that we have not confined it to this sphere. Can the story of American education be told apart from the story of wealth? or the story of our advancing aesthetic interests? or even the story of religion? It would be foolish to pretend that moneymakers sought wealth simply to build churches, finance art galleries, or endow universities; business motivation cannot be reduced to such simple, idealistic terms. But it is equally unrealistic to ignore the fact that the quest for money has often had consequences beyond the realm of the material.

Nor is the assertion that the American measures success by the yardstick of wealth anything more than a half truth. If success consists simply of power and fame, wealth will buy both, but when we find elements of creativeness and self-realization in the careers of men who conquer fortune, such a definition becomes hopelessly inadequate. Does our yardstick of success exclude such elements as "doing good to others," the attainment of happiness, and the winning of salvation? The American does not believe so, and he will argue that a man can accomplish more good with money than without it, that money is practically a prerequisite for happiness, and that he has heard clergymen say that no man is more pleasing unto God than the morally upright millionaire. He may even feel a trace of patriotic pride in his material success. Where but in America is there such an abundance of opportunity? Where, except under our institutions, is the individual so free to work out his economic destiny? Where has the nobody so often become somebody on the strength of his personal powers?

The legendary hero of America is the self-made man. He has been active in every field from politics to the arts, but nowhere has he been more active, or more acclaimed, than in business. To most Americans he is the office boy who has become the head of a great concern, making millions in the process. He represents our most cherished conceptions of success, and particularly our belief that any man can achieve fortune through the practice of industry, frugality, and sobriety.

The pages which follow attempt to explore the story

of the rags-to-riches idea in terms of its practical relation to our business civilization. They attempt to explain the origin, nature, and content of the idea; something of its relation to religion, education, and general movements of thought; something of its propagation, and its social uses; and something of the men who loved and despised the idea. The doctrine of self-help is simple and unsophisticated, more at home with ordinary men than with philosophers. Its history is not the history of a great abstraction, but the saga of an idea that had power among the people.

These pages do not pretend to chronicle the lives of self-made men, or to settle the question of how many American millionaires were self-made and how many were not. Nor do they pretend to explain the methods and practices which enabled men to conquer fortune. We will be concerned here not with business history but intellectual history, and specifically with the realm of ideas about self-help under American conditions of opportunity.

In the Beginning

IN THE NATION'S CAPITAL on June 29, 1869, the graduating class of the Spencerian Business College assembled for final exercises. The speaker for the occasion was a politician, but he did not talk about Reconstruction, or any other current political issue. Instead, James A. Garfield took up a matter of more personal concern to both his audience and himself, the problem of getting ahead in the world. He asserted that in the aristocracies of the Old World, where society was stratified like the rocks of the earth, it was uncommon for a boy to rise from the lowest to the highest social strata, but in America, where society was as fluid as the ocean, poor boys continually rose to displace those riding the crests. This, he declared, was the chief glory of America.[1] Twelve years later James A. Garfield became President of the United States. His own rise from a log cabin to the White House offered proof of his thesis.

To the young men of the Spencerian Business College Garfield's message could scarcely qualify as news. They were already familiar with the tradition of log-cabin Presidents, and their choice of business vocations suggested an equal knowledge, and perhaps greater admiration, of the careers of such men as John Jacob Astor, Peter Cooper, and Cornelius Vanderbilt. The truth was that even before the Civil War there was considerable worship of self-made men of wealth, and a widespread desire to emulate them. In 1853 *Harper's New Monthly Magazine* reported that to the vast majority of Americans success had long since come to mean achievement in business, and in making money. "The idea instilled into the minds of most boys, from early life," the article declared, "is that of 'getting on.' The parents test themselves by their own success in this respect; and they impart the same notion to their children." [2] Parents had no monopoly on this idea, of course, for writers and orators characteristically loved the rags-to-riches theme and helped to spread it widely. At mid-century the young man who went to church, or to the lyceum, or to the reading rooms of a mercantile library association was bound to hear or read something about the self-made man and his glorious conquest of fortune.

The popular American conception of this phenomenon was much narrower, however, than the dictionary definition which described the self-made man as one who had achieved success in any work without benefit of external advantages, one who had risen from obscurity on the strength of personal merit. Although the dictionary allowed the self-made artist, writer, or clergyman as much honor as the titan of trade, it is a matter of record that actually they were not so highly honored, or so widely worshipped. "Analyze the elements of it," an English observer wrote in 1885, "and you will see that success is identified to some extent with fame; still more with power; most of all, with wealth." [3] And it was not to men of the professions but to a group of successful manufacturers that the term "self-made men" was first applied. On February 2, 1832, Henry Clay was defending the protective tariff in the Senate against charges of his Southern opponents that a tariff would spawn an hereditary industrial aristocracy. Not so, Clay replied. A protective tariff would widen opportunities and enable humble men to rise in the industrial sphere. "In Kentucky," he said, "almost every manufactory known to me is in the hands of enterprising self-made men, who have whatever wealth they possess by patient and diligent labor." [4]

II

Though it was an American conceit that the self-made man was peculiar to our shores, he had been known in other lands. Since virtually all societies provided some channels for vertical social circulation, men of this type had been common to all. In the older nations of Europe such institutions as the army, the church, the school, and the political party served as agencies for testing, sifting, and distributing individuals within various social strata. Even in associating the self-made man with wealth America enjoyed no special distinction, for in ancient Greece and Rome successful moneymakers often rose into the ruling class, regardless of social origin. And in the Italian city-states and the commercial centers of Western Europe at the close of the Middle Ages moneymaking was one of the most common and omnipotent means of social promotion.[5]

Seventeenth-century England was especially familiar with the economic definition applied to this class of men, for as the English merchant classes rose to power they inspired a substantial literature of justification. Publicists associated with the English business community turned out many pamphlets, sermons, and guidebooks which pointed out the way to wealth. One of these English classics was Richard Johnson's *Nine Worthies of London* (1592), an account of nine apprentices who rose to positions of honor through the exercise of personal virtue. Another of these handbooks, *A Treatise of the Vocations* (1603), written by William Perkins, a learned Cambridge theologian, was held in special regard by Americans. In the seventeenth century success-minded immigrants sometimes carried Perkins' book with them to the New World, and read it for guidance and inspiration.[6] Of course the great majority who came to America had no room for books, but they doubtless carried in their heads an ample store of self-help homilies, for such maxims were common coin in England.

It is a commonplace of American colonial history that most immigrants came to the New World in the hope of improving their economic status. The agricultural laborer knew that land here was plentiful, and easily acquired, while tradesmen and day laborers built their hopes around the prospect of the high wages which were a natural consequence of the scarcity of labor. On every side American opportunities damaged class patterns inherited from Europe, and altered old orders of caste and custom. In a land where achievement was more important than titles of nobility there was always the possibility that a nobody could become a man of consequence if he worked hard and kept his eye on the main chance. Ralph Barton Perry put it very well when, speaking of colonial artisans and tradesmen, he observed that "They were neither so unfortunate as to be imbued with a sense of helplessness, nor so privileged as to be satisfied with their present status. They possessed just enough to whet their appetites for more and to feel confident of their power to attain it." [7]

After the starving time had passed and commercial

towns had sprung up along the Atlantic seaboard, urban dwellers could dream not just of competence but of wealth. Cadwallader Colden, reporting on New York City in 1748, asserted that "The only principle of life propagated among the young people is to get money, and men are only esteemed according to what they are worth—that is, the money they are possessed of." [8] This passion for wealth was one which enjoyed the sanction of religion, especially in New England, where Puritan clergymen assured their congregations that God approved business callings, and rewarded virtue with wealth. Cotton Mather, for example, in *Two Brief Discourses, one Directing a Christian in his General Calling; another Directing him in his Personal Calling* (1701) taught that in addition to serving Christ, which was man's general calling, all men were obliged to succeed in some useful secular employment, in order to win salvation in this life as well as in the next. In *Essays To Do Good* (1710) he argued that prosperity was the gift of God, and that men of wealth were God's stewards, charged with the responsibility of doing good to their fellows.[9] Such doctrines as these, inherited from seventeenth-century England, occupied a central place in the American success rationale.

It was no accident that the best-known colonial self-made man was Benjamin Franklin, a product of Puritan Boston. At a tender age he read Cotton Mather's *Essays To Do Good,* later crediting them with having had a profound and lifelong influence on his thought and conduct. He also received advice from his father, a humble Puritan candlemaker, who drummed into his head the meaning of the ancient proverb: "Seest thou a man diligent in his business? He shall stand before kings." Fortified by these principles of self-help Franklin migrated to Philadelphia, the Quaker commercial metropolis, to begin his rise in the printing trade. The story of his upward climb has always enjoyed a prominent place in the folklore of success. Through *Poor Richard's Almanack* (1732–1757) he publicized prosperity maxims which have probably exerted as much practical influence on Americans as the combined teachings of all the formal philosophers. Certainly in the nineteenth century the alleged virtues of the American people closely resembled the virtues of Poor Richard.[10]

During the American Revolution Franklin's energies were diverted into other channels, and it was the third decade of the nineteenth century before his self-help themes were revived by a new generation of success propagandists. In the troubled years after 1763 publicists were too busy framing assertions of political independence, too busy contriving Federalist and Republican polemics, to be diverted to the writing of maxims of trade. And despite the gains made in industry, commerce, and finance between the Revolution and the period of Jackson's rise to power, few prophets arose to call young men to action in these spheres. By 1830, however, the impacts of the Industrial Revolution could no longer be ignored; in the great cities of the North and East, journalists, clergymen, lawyers and other spokesmen began to lay the foundations for the powerful nineteenth-century cult of the self-made man.

III

Appropriately Benjamin Franklin became the first object of adoration in this cult, the convenient symbol which linked the success traditions of the two centuries.

In 1826 Simeon Ide, a Vermont printer, dedicated a new edition of Franklin's *The Way to Wealth* and *Advice to Young Tradesmen* to the mechanics and farmers of New England. He urged every workingman to reflect on his own advantages, and to compare them with the disadvantages that Franklin had encountered, observing that "Perhaps he may, from a comparison, draw the conclusion, that he has greater advantages in his favour, and fewer discouragements to encounter, than had the persevering Franklin. If this be really the case, what other impediment can there be in his way . . . but the want of a resolute determination to merit, by a similar conduct, the good fortune which attended him?" [11] Ide urged any youth who aspired to wealth or station to lean on the counsel and example of Franklin where he might hope to find an almost infallible passport to the ultimatum of his wishes.

At Boston in 1831 a series of Franklin Lectures was begun with the avowed object of inspiring the young men of that city to make the most of their opportunities. Edward Everett inaugurated the series, proclaiming that the story of Franklin's rise could not be told too often. The most successful men in history, he declared, had been men "of humble origin, narrow fortunes, small advantages, and self-taught." [12] Twenty-six years later, when a statue of Franklin was unveiled in Boston, Robert C. Winthrop again used the occasion to arouse the working class from their lethargy:

> Behold him, Mechanics and Mechanics' Apprentices, holding out to you an example of diligence, economy and virtue, and personifying the triumphant success which may await those who follow it! Behold him, ye that are humblest and poorest in present condition or in future prospect,—

> lift up your heads and look at the image of a man who rose from nothing, who owed nothing to parentage or patronage, who enjoyed no advantages of early education which are not open,—a hundred fold open,—to yourselves, who performed the most menial services in the business in which his early life was employed, but who lived to stand before Kings, and died to leave a name which the world will never forget.[13]

Probably the number of poor boys who were actually inspired to great deeds by the example of Franklin was never large, but at least one, Thomas Mellon, founder of a great banking fortune, has testified to the influence of Franklin on his life. In the year 1828 young Mellon, then fourteen years old, was living on a farm outside the rising industrial city of Pittsburgh. After he had read a battered copy of Franklin's *Autobiography* which he had picked up at a neighbor's house, he found himself aflame with a new ambition. "I had not before imagined," he said, "any other course of life superior to farming, but the reading of Franklin's life led me to question this view. For so poor and friendless a boy to be able to become a merchant or a professional man had before seemed an impossibility; but here was Franklin, poorer than myself, who by industry, thrift and frugality had become learned and wise, and elevated to wealth and fame. The maxims of 'Poor Richard' exactly suited my sentiments. . . . I regard the reading of Franklin's *Autobiography* as the turning point of my life." [14] Abandoning the family farm at Poverty Point young Mellon migrated to Pittsburgh, where he made his way as a lawyer and money lender. Later when he had founded his own bank it was Franklin's statue that he placed at the front of the building as a symbol of his inspiration, and in the last years of his life he bought a thousand copies of Franklin's *Autobiography,* which he distributed to young men who came seeking advice and money.

Important though Franklin was as a symbol and inspiration, the magnificent economic opportunities of nineteenth-century America constituted a far more important inspiration to young men in quest of wealth. The urge to get ahead was especially strong in areas which had been transformed by the Industrial Revolution; it was no accident that three out of every four nineteenth-century millionaires were natives of New England, New York, or Pennsylvania, and that 70 percent won their fortunes in either manufacturing, banking, trade, or transportation.[15] Such activities were concentrated in the cities, in old commercial centers like New York, Philadelphia, and Boston, or in new industrial towns such as Lawrence, Lowell, Rochester, and Pittsburgh, cities which held the key to fortune for the ambitious poor. On the eve of the Civil War it was a backward metropolis indeed that could not boast of its self-made businessmen, and an American who knew nothing of the careers of Amos and Abbott Lawrence, Samuel Appleton, John Jacob Astor, Peter Cooper, Cornelius Vanderbilt, Stephen Girard, or George Peabody was considered hopelessly uninformed.

In and near the great urban centers sensitive observers divined the tendency of the age and gave it their sanction. "How widely spread is the passion for acquisition," exulted William Ellery Channing of Boston, "not for simple means of subsistence, but for wealth! What vast enterprises agitate the community! What a rush into all the departments of trade." [16] As Channing saw it, it was this tendency that explained the progressive vigor of America in the 1840s. Ralph Waldo Emerson agreed. This philosopher who preached self-reliance also pronounced benedictions on those single-minded businessmen who created the wealth that raised man above the subsistence level, blessed him with leisure, and gave him access to the masterworks of the human race. "The pulpit and the press have many commonplaces denouncing the thirst for wealth," said Emerson; "but if men should take these moralists at their word and leave off aiming to be rich, the moralists would rush to rekindle at all hazards this love of power in the people, lest civilization should be undone." [17]

As a good Boston Brahmin Oliver Wendell Holmes was no special friend of business upstarts, but even he conceded that America could be justly proud of those self-made men who had come forward before the Civil War to form a new aristocracy. He thought this aristocracy was "very splendid, though its origin may have been tar, tallow, train-oil, or other such unctuous commodities." [18] Moreover, he believed that after ten years of patient and diligent labor any enterprising young man might rise into this elite. Holmes was not alone in this estimate, for John Aiken, an observer of industrial conditions at Lowell, Massachusetts, reported in 1849 that "He who five years ago was working for wages, will now be found transacting business for himself, and a few years hence, will be likely to be found a hirer of the labor of others." [19]

In New York, no less than in New England, the glories of accumulation and the precepts of self-help were widely trumpeted. In 1842 the editor of the New York *Sun,* Moses Yale Beach, gave Americans their first directory of men distinguished chiefly for their possession of money when he published his famous *Wealth and Pedigree of the Wealthy Citizens of New York City.* He tried to include all local men worth a hundred thousand dollars or more; at the top of his list of fourteen millionaires he placed the name of John Jacob Astor, a self-made German immigrant, with a fortune estimated at ten million.[20] In order to benefit his readers Beach called attention to those "who by honest and laborious industry have raised themselves from the obscure walks of life, to great wealth and consideration," and singled out "some of the brightest examples of prosperity in this *touch-stone* land as beacons for those ambitious of fortune's favors." [21]

Beach had strong competition in this field of publicity in the person of Freeman Hunt, a migrant from Massachusetts who, after locating in New York, began to report the triumphs of American merchants. *Hunt's Merchants' Magazine,* founded in 1839, tried to inform the world of the merchant's doings and of his usefulness to mankind. As publisher of this journal Hunt collected thousands of business anecdotes and maxims of trade which he turned to good account in *Worth and Wealth* (1856), a compilation that established him as a worthy successor to Benjamin Franklin. Two years later he published a two-volume *Lives of American Merchants* (1858), which explained the rules of success through the lives of men who had achieved it.

Philadelphia too had self-help prophets to match those of New York and Boston in pointing the way to wealth. Philadelphia's counterpart of Freeman Hunt was Edwin Troxell Freedley, a prolific writer who served manufacturers as Hunt served merchants. Freedley's *Practical Treatise on Business* (1852) rivalled Hunt's *Worth and Wealth* in popularity, and his *Leading Pursuits and Leading Men* (1856) was on the market two years before

Hunt's *Lives of American Merchants* was offered for sale. Another Philadelphian who popularized themes of business triumph was Timothy Shay Arthur, onetime watchmaker's apprentice, counting room clerk, and bank agent. Though his fame rested primarily on *Ten Nights in a Barroom* (1854), Arthur was also well known for his self-help homilies, and for his demand for a new kind of American biography. "In this country," he asserted, "the most prominent and efficient men are not those who were born to wealth and eminent social positions, but those who have won both by the force of untiring personal energy. It is to them that the country is indebted for unbounded prosperity. Invaluable, therefore, are the lives of such men to the rising generation. . . . Hitherto, American Biography has confined itself too closely to men who have won political or literary distinction. . . . Limited to the perusal of such biographies, our youth must, of necessity, receive erroneous impressions of the true construction of our society, and fail to perceive wherein the progressive vigor of the nation lies. . . . We want the histories of our self-made men spread out before us, that we may know the ways by which they came up from the ranks of the people." [22] Within two years Arthur's demand had been met in the form of Charles C. B. Seymour's *Self-Made Men* (1858), an inspiring account of poor boys who had made their mark in the world.

On the eve of the Civil War this rags-to-riches theme had already captured the imagination of young men living close to the centers of business enterprise. A New York clergyman observed that "Their plans, their thoughts, their energies, are, day and night, concentrated to this one point, to become opulent, the sooner the better." [23] This was the appealing dream, born of the opportunities of the urban frontier and nourished by a rising army of self-help propagandists. In the days before Sumter the counting room clerk and the bobbin boy dreamed more of private fortune than of military glory. And though the Civil War imposed military values on the nation, it did so only temporarily. Out of the war came rich new opportunities for acquisition, a new generation of self-made men, and a well-ordered gospel of business success.

As the Twig Is Bent

II

WHAT MAKES THE MAN? Is he shaped by conditions that surround him, or by forces inherent in himself? Through the long history of American thinking on the subject of success no questions have been more central, and none have been answered more confidently. To the generation that sired Andrew Carnegie and John D. Rockefeller the relation of a favorable economic environment to personal fortune should have been obvious. And sometimes it was. P. T. Barnum, for example, admitted that "In a new country, where we have more land than people, it is not at all difficult for persons in good health to make money."[1] But most prophets of success refused to tell their tales in terms of the favorable ratio of men to resources, preferring instead to talk about how character could triumph over circumstance. "The things which are really essential for a successful life are not circumstances, but qualities," one spokesman said, "not the things which surround a man, but the things which are in him; not the adjuncts of his position, but the attributes of his character."[2] This had to be the emphasis, of course, for otherwise there could be no such social being as a self-made man.

In minimizing the role of the economic environment advocates of self-help did not, however, dismiss it entirely. They simply insisted that American opportunities were so plentiful, and so open to all, that each and every man could make as much of himself as he desired. "The road to fortune, like the public turnpike, is open alike to the children of the beggar, and the descendant of kings," one adviser declared. "There are tolls to be paid by all, yet all have rights, and it only remains for us to avail ourselves of these." [3] It was a matter of common agreement that never in the history of the world had chances for success been greater than in post–Civil-War America. As Horace Greeley told an audience of young hopefuls at the Cooper Union in 1867, "There is in this land of ours larger opportunities, more just and well grounded hopes, than any other land whereon the sun ever shone." [4] In less fortunate lands men might behold success from afar and worship it, but few could dream of achieving it. Here on the other hand the attainment of fame and fortune was a common expectation.

How could this be? In America was there not inequality in the land, and more poverty than wealth? True, the apostles of self-help admitted, but this condition forced the young to struggle against adversity and thus furnished the very means by which they might develop the qualities necessary for success. "It is the struggle which develops," said an authority on self-help, "—the effort to redeem one's self from iron surroundings;—which calls out manhood and unfolds womanhood to the highest possibilities." [5] In the religion of success poverty became the equivalent of sin in Calvinist theology, an evil to be struggled against and overcome. The greater the poverty out of which a man climbed, the greater the testimony to the force of his character. According to this reasoning, those who would be least likely to succeed would be the children of the rich, for without struggle against adversity they would be deprived of the means of developing the necessary strength of character. This was what Henry Ward Beecher tried to convey to the wealthy merchants of Brooklyn's Plymouth Church when he told them that their financial losses might be their children's gain. "How blessed, then, is the stroke of disaster which sets the children free, and gives them over to the hard but kind bosom of Poverty, who says to them, 'Work!' and, working, makes them men." [6]

Among business enterprisers the stoutest defender of the advantages of poverty was Andrew Carnegie, who insisted that practically all the titans of his generation has been trained in poverty's stern but efficient school. "They appear upon the stage, athletes trained for the contest, with sinews braced, indomitable wills, resolved to do or die. Such boys always have marched, and always will march, straight to the front and lead the world; they are the epochmakers." [7] Society could ill afford to be without poverty, Carnegie argued, for without poverty there would be no extraordinary men, and without extraordinary men there could be no social progress. "Abolish luxury, if you please," he said, "but leave us the soil, upon which alone the virtues and all that is precious in human character grow; poverty—honest poverty." [8]

In defending poverty Carnegie was not simply justifying maldistribution of wealth under a capitalist economy. He was also romanticizing the circumstances which had surrounded his own childhood and that of many other business leaders of his generation. Just how many of these wealthy men of the nineteenth century actually did rise from poverty we shall probably never know, but there have been some informed guesses. In his study of deceased American millionaires, mostly men of the last century, Pitirim Sorokin, for example, discovered that 38.8 percent of them started life poor. Another statistical study of the American business elite showed that 43 percent of those leaders who came to maturity around the year 1870 originated in the lower classes; they encountered fewer difficulties on their road from rags to riches than earlier or later generations. From a strictly statistical point of view, around 1835 appears to have been the most propitious birth year for a poor boy who hoped to rise into the business elite.[9] Carnegie hit it right on the mark, for he was born in 1835 and came to his business maturity after the Civil War. With the evidence around him, it is not surprising that he should have sensed that in his generation, more than ever before, poor boys were on the march. And what was more natural than his attempts and those of other self-made men to discover in the poverty of their youth the source of their later strength?

II

Along with the glorification of poverty in the success cult's ideology went the glorification of rural childhood. Throughout the last century self-help propagandists insisted that rural origins foretold success and urban origins failure. It is not difficult to understand the basis for such assertions for it is an historic fact that the great cities of the nineteenth century were built up, in part at least, by migrations from rural areas, and that the country boy sometimes did rise into the ranks of the urban business elite. Philip D. Armour, James J. Hill,

Collis P. Huntington, Cornelius Vanderbilt, Daniel Drew, and Jay Gould all came from the farm. Self-help publicists needed only a hasty glance at the rolls of wealth to convince themselves that there must be some cause and effect relationship between country origins and the qualities that enabled a man to conquer fortune. As Orison Marden noted, "The sturdy, vigorous, hardy qualities, the stamina, the brawn, the grit which characterize men who do great things in this world, are, as a rule, country bred." [10]

One of the favorite migrations of ambitious country boys was from New England to the urban centers of New York and Pennsylvania. Because of its accessibility New York City was especially attractive to boys from back-country New England. In the years after 1820 they swarmed into the rising metropolis, captured it, and dominated its business life until after the Civil War.[11] "All do not succeed," a contemporary reported, "but some do, and this is quite sufficient to keep the ambition to get a clerkship in New York alive." [12] Joseph A. Scoville, who knew as much as any man about the New York business community at mid-century, thought there was no mystery about the country boy's rise to positions of leadership. "He needs but a foothold," said Scoville. "He asks no more . . . wherever this boy strikes, he fastens." According to Scoville New York merchants preferred to hire country boys, on the theory that they worked harder, and were more resolute, obedient, and cheerful than native New Yorkers. Too often city boys objected to menial tasks, complaining that they were intended for better things. Nothing, not even the blackening of the employer's boots, was beneath the dignity of the New Englander.[13] Presumably this attitude went far towards explaining his rapid rise.

It would be difficult to say how many farmers' sons thus won fame and fortune but there is little doubt that contemporaries exaggerated their number. In 1883 a Brooklyn clergyman, Wilbur F. Crafts, published the results of his investigations of the lives of five hundred successful Americans representing all lines of endeavor. According to his data 57 percent of the successful men of his day were born in the country, and only 17 percent in the city. "The first conclusion from these facts," said Crafts, "is that a man who wishes to succeed should select a country farm for his birthplace. . . ."[14] Another study, published in 1909, showed that out of 47 railroad presidents who answered questions about their origins, 55.4 percent came from farms or villages.[15] Three more recent surveys, however, point toward the opposite direction. Farm boys accounted for only 24.6 percent of the deceased American millionaires investigated by Sorokin; only 23.8 percent of the elite businessmen whose origins were checked by C. Wright Mills; and only 12 percent of the twentieth-century leaders studied by William Miller.[16] Even so, as a group farmers' sons ranked second only to the sons of businessmen in the achievement of outstanding success. This and the fact that farm boys started with fewer advantages made them the favorite candidates for heroes in the cult of the self-made man.

The alleged advantages of rural beginnings concerned mostly health and morals. Fresh air and good food kept the country boy in good physical condition, and his daily round of work left him little time for the mischief that distracted his less busy city cousin. Whereas city boys wasted their lives and their substance in saloons, gambling dens, and houses of prostitution, country boys supposedly led a Spartan life that prepared them for the hard struggle of the business world. "Our successful men did not feed themselves on boyhood cigarettes and late suppers, with loafing as their only labor, and midnight parties for their regular evening dissipation," a clergyman declared in 1883. "Such city-trained bodies often give out when the strain comes in business, while the sound body and mind and morals of the man from the country hold on and hold out." [17] In 1909 President Louis W. Hill of the Great Northern Railway testified that, despite the personal inconvenience involved, he had chosen to live on a farm rather than in the city in order to give his three boys the best possible start in life. "I believe," said Hill, "there is no end of arguments that living on the farm gives the best chance for a growing boy." [18]

In only one respect, and that a crucial one, did philosophers of success concede that cities offered advantages which rural villages could not match. Opportunities for making money, they agreed, were better in the city. If the farm boy expected to become a millionaire he had to migrate to a metropolis. Even the most insensitive observers seemed to understand that the road to fortune must pass through the city. Many self-help handbooks therefore encouraged farm boys to leave home. "A boy at home seldom has a chance," said one blunt adviser. "Nobody believes in him,—least of all his relations." [19] Out of deference to parents most writers tried to be more subtle; instead of telling boys to leave home they advised them indirectly to do so by talking about the importance of setting up in the right location. "No man can expect to become distinguished in any sphere unless he has the amplest field for the exercise of his powers," one handbook declared. "A. T. Stewart located anywhere out of New York City, would not be what he is, and many a clergyman or lawyer, fixed in a small village, would not have reached the eminence which the world freely accords them." [20] It was sad, but true, that if a country boy desired fortune he had to leave home to achieve it. If there was any consolation in this uprooting, it was in the conviction that his chance of failure was slight so long as he remained faithful to the virtues that formed his country character.

III

When the boy ventured into the world his memories of home and mother were supposed to be a source of powerful influence on his future. Poverty and rural surroundings might school him in virtue, but the schooling was often harsh. Not so with the lessons learned at a mother's knee. Of all the external influences leading young men into the byways of success, none had greater honor in the cult of self-help than that of mother. "The testimony of great men in acknowledgment of the boundless debt they owe to their mothers would make a record stretching from the dawn of history to to-day," said a a high priest of the cult. "Few men indeed, become great who do not owe their greatness to a mother's love and inspiration." [21] In the case of successful moneymakers, mothers deserved credit not because of any instruction in the ways of business, but because of their role of molding the character on which business achievement was supposed to depend. As Albert J. Beveridge remarked, American mothers trained their sons in honor rather than success, but success was the inevitable by-product.[22]

Granting this power of mothers, it was fortunate that there were no irresponsibles among those described in the literature of success. "I can not imagine a better woman than my mother," said Philip D. Armour in typical testimony. "My childhood was ideal. God did not overlook me." [23]

According to most self-help advocates a young man who moved away from his parental home was not doomed thereby to lose forever the blessings of female comfort and counsel, for they assumed that a young man with ambition would marry. "Marry a true woman, and have your own home," was an oft-repeated exhortation. The young businessman who desired a good name, they cautioned, would do well to marry, because a good wife would be the means of saving him from loose women, gambling, drink, and other vices which damaged reputation. In addition, they argued, the married man was morally superior to the bachelor, and therefore preferred by both creditors and employers.[24]

It should be noted, however, that the young businessman who married in order to improve his success did not choose his wife on the basis of her material possessions. In the theory of success money was to be earned, not married, and he who married for money was engaging in dangerous speculation, for the heiress was quite likely to be indolent and extravagant. "With the very best of purposes she does not know how to adapt herself to a mode of life less expensive than that which obtained in her father's house, and her inheritance alone is rarely ever sufficient for that." [25]

The good wife enriched her husband by bringing profitable qualities of character, not money, into the home. She was economical, hard-working, orderly, neat, steady, and firm in disposition. She was never extravagant, because "An extravagant wife is an injury to a merchant's credit." [26] She was cheerful, especially in hard times, and never addicted to nagging. The nagging wife was a millstone about her husband's neck, making him useless to himself, his employer, and to the world. "I have seen more men fail in business through the attitude taken by their wives . . . than from all the vices put together," Charles M. Schwab testified. "A nagging wife . . . is one of the worst handicaps he could have." [27] The wife who gave her husband kindness and affection enriched him also with wealth:

I came to the desk where old Commerce grew grey,
And asked him what helped him this many a day,
In his old smoky room with his ledger to stay?
And it all was the beauty,
The comfort and duty,
That cheered him at home.[28]

In point of fact, successful moneymakers were married men more often than not. Almost 97 percent of the millionares of the nineteenth century were married, and 94 percent of those of the twentieth century. In each of these eras wealthy men ranked well above the average for adult males in the matter of taking vows.[29] Undoubtedly the millionaire's financial status contributed much to his eligibility, but this was a point that prophets of success were reluctant to concede. "They are not married men because they are better off than their fellows," said one authority, "but are better off because they are married men." [30] This bordered on doctrinal heresy, of course, for if it were admitted that a wife held the key to her husband's success, what then became of the self-made man?

Whenever self-help theorists touched on the roles played by the economic environment, by rural upbringing, or by wives and mothers, they always had to be wary lest they attribute too much to these external influences. Sound doctrine demanded that explanations for success be found within the man and not outside him. As Emerson remarked, "the reason why this or that man is fortunate is not to be told. It lies in the man; that is all anybody can tell you about it." [31] Long after Emerson's passing a more practical philosopher, Henry Ford, reiterated the same point. "The law of success is in the person himself," said Ford. "What is the law by which the apple becomes an apple? Well, it's the same way with success." [32]

By the same token the causes of failure lay within the man. Every year after 1890 the firm of Dun and Bradstreet analyzed the business failures of the preceding year in terms of the personal and impersonal factors involved. Invariably the greater number of failures were explained by such categories as incompetence, inexperience, extravagance, fraud, and neglect. Only infrequently were failures charged against depressed business conditions or other causes beyond the control of the individual. After surveying the causes of failure thus reported for the period 1902–1910, one self-help theorist concluded that "Long years of experience have demonstrated to the seekers after the underlying causes of business failure the fact that, generally speaking four-fifths of all failures are due to faults inherent in the person, while about one-fifth are due to causes outside and beyond his control. . . . In other words, the cool, disinterested judgment of thousands of investigators shows that success or failure largely lies within the person himself rather than with outside conditions." [33] In all times and places this was the doctrine which identified true prophets of the cult of the self-made man.

The Power Within

III

HE WHO IS INTERESTED in the relation of business methods to business success will find little elucidation in the rags-to-riches literature of the nineteenth century. Most of these self-help handbooks offer little practical advice on advertising methods, accounting systems, investment procedures, production techniques, and other such mundane matters. Technical considerations are quite remote from their main discussion which revolves around private character and morality. What profited it a man to master all the skills of trade if he had not first mastered himself? At best, successful methods were merely by-products of successful character. The businessman who had the right personal qualities would have little difficulty in developing the necessary managerial skills, but the possession of no amount of skill could compensate for lack of character or other essential personal traits. So ran the argument.

In considering the inner qualities that make for success self-help theorists minimized the importance of talents that were inherited rather than cultivated. Economic salvation, like spiritual salvation, was not reserved for men of superior physique and intellect, but could be attained by all men of good character. In respect to character, presumably, all started as equals. It was not the boast of the self-made man that nature had made him stronger and more intelligent than his fellows, it was that through the cultivation of good character he had managed his own elevation. As Theodore Roosevelt remarked, in explaining success, "no brilliancy of intellect, no perfection of bodily development will count when weighed in the balance against that assemblage of virtues . . . which we group together under the name of character." [1]

To the great majority not endowed with genius the success gospel offered the comforting assurance that no high order of intelligence was required of the businessman. This assurance was heard with special frequency before 1890, in the years when opportunity seemed limitless, and there were few giant corporations to restrict chances for the average man.[2] The genius, like the college man, was usually described as lazy, vain, impatient, and undisciplined, a man who sought a conspicuous place, a short work, and a large reward. Henry Ward Beecher, notorious for his dullness as a boy, touched on a common theme when he analyzed the genius for an audience of young men at Indianapolis in 1844. "So far as my observations have ascertained the species," he said, "they abound in academies, colleges, and Thespian societies; in village debating clubs; in coteries of young artists, and young professional aspirants. They are to be known by a reserved air, excessive sensitiveness, and utter indolence; by very long hair, and very open shirt collars; by the reading of much wretched poetry, and the writing of much, yet more wretched; by being very conceited, very affected, very disagreeable, and very useless:—beings whom no man wants for friend, pupil, or companion." [3] Beecher did not stand alone in this estimate. In 1878 Albert Rhodes, the American consul at Rouen, France, writing in defense of the "successful mediocrity" for the *International Review,* asserted that geniuses were irregular in the performance of duty, imprudent in word and deed, poorly married, and worst of all, poor of purse. William Holmes McGuffey tried to explain to his youthful readers that the trouble with the genius was that he relied too much on his natural powers, and too little on the cultivated qualities that win success:

Thus, plain, plodding people, we often shall find,
Will leave hasty, confident people behind:
Like the tortoise and hare, though together they start,
We soon clearly see they are widely apart.

While one trusts the gifts Dame Nature bestows,
And relying on these, calmly stops for repose,
The other holds slowly and surely his way,
And thus wins the race, ere the close of the day.

From Ralph Waldo Emerson to Orison Marden experts on moneymaking agreed that genius was not only not required; it was not even desirable. Emerson's observations led him to believe that the right man for business was that just-average man who had an abundance of common sense. The business community itself echoed this sentiment. "There is no genius required," said James D. Mills, a New York merchant. "And if there were, some great men have said that genius is no more than common-sense intensified." [4] Presumably the businessman needed an orderly and methodical mind, an affinity for facts, a sound memory, good judgment, and mathematical skill. Theodore Parker summarized the necessary requirements when he analyzed Amos Lawrence as a careful, methodical, diligent man, and one of very ordinary intellect. "He had no uncommon culture of the understanding or the imagination," Parker observed, "and of the higher reason still less. But in respect of the greater faculties—in respect of conscience, affection, the religious element—he was well born, well bred, eminently well disciplined by himself." [5] Others who reflected on these matters argued that in the business world, at least, perseverance and industry could accomplish far more than genius. "The genius which has accomplished great things in the world, as a rule, is the genius for downright hard work, persistent drudgery," Orison Marden declared. "This is the genius that has transformed the world, and led civilization from the rude devices of the Hottentots to the glorious achievements of our own century." [6]

If self-help advocates deprecated genius, they thought better of other gifts of nature, particularly the specialized talents or aptitudes. In keeping with the dominant faculty psychology of the nineteenth century most success theorists assumed that the human mind consisted of many separate faculties, each of which could be improved through conscious effort. Presumably every man had special faculties which, if properly cultivated, would help him win outstanding success in his chosen field. According to Orison Marden, God organized man's whole anatomy for the purpose of achievement. Every cell, nerve, and fiber had its special role to play. "The Creator made man a success-machine," he declared, "and failure is as abnormal to him as discord is to harmony." [7] God did not intend all men for business, of course, or for any other single vocation. Provision had to be made for all useful occupations and was accomplished through the distribution of diverse faculties among men. The discovery, development, and application of these faculties added up to the success of the individual and the welfare of the world.

The special faculty of the businessman equipped him to make money, for he was peculiarly endowed with what a Chicago financial editor described as "the organ of acquisitiveness." [8] Sooner or later he would feel the faculty of business stirring within him and know that he had been called to a lifetime of accumulation. Once called, it was a sin for him to turn aside from the career for which God had prepared him. Authorities on success warned continually against misinterpreting, resisting, or ignoring one's natural bent respecting a vocation. Those who erred in this respect invited failure, for "Unless a man enters upon a vocation intended for him by nature, and best suited to his peculiar genius, he cannot succeed . . . we see many who have mistaken their calling, from the blacksmith up (or down) to the clergyman. You will see, for instance, the 'learned blacksmith,' who ought to have been a teacher of languages; and you may have seen lawyers, doctors, and clergymen who were better fitted by nature for the anvil or the lapstone." [9]

In this, as in all other matters, the ambitious youth was supposed to be self-reliant, for no one could know him as well as he knew himself. Every young man was supposed to study his interests and abilities in relation to the requirements of the various vocations, and on this basis make a decision regarding his life's work. If after much self-analysis the issue was still in doubt, the nineteenth-century youth was sometimes advised to turn to a phrenologist for counsel. In 1873 a New York medical doctor, Joseph Simms, urged ambitious boys to "seek the counsel of a professional physiognomist," on the ground that phrenologists could predict "with complete scientific accuracy" the vocation in which a youth would prosper.[10] By writing guidebooks to success, nationally known phrenologists such as Samuel Wells and Nelson Sizer extended their knowledge to those who could not visit their parlors for personal readings. It is doubtful, however, that their advice differed very extensively from the counsel of clergymen, journalists, and businessmen.

Self-help theorists generally agreed that self-analysis did not end with the discovery of one's general calling. Within each calling there were specialties, and the man who aimed for the highest success had to cultivate one of these. Rural America had honored versatility, cherishing the Jack-of-all-trades above the expert, but the demands of urban life reversed this system of values. As businesses grew in size and complexity in the years after the Civil War the highly specialized man became the darling of the success cult. "Silly men may cry out against one-idead men," an adviser wrote in 1878, "but very seldom have men with two ideas accomplished any creditable work." [11] Competition was so severe, time so short, and human energy so limited, that no man could win fortune if he divided his efforts among several enterprises. "Knowledge is now so various, so extensive, and so minute," said Andrew Carnegie, "that it is impossible for any man to know thoroughly more than one small branch." [12] Carnegie spoke for the entire school of success experts when he advised young men to put all their eggs in one basket, and then watch the basket.

Advice on specialization, like all other advice offered by success counselors, was meaningless if considered apart from the all-powerful human will, the most important of God's gifts to man. What use to advise if man had no power to remodel himself along profitable lines? Behind the success cult's exhortations lay the assumption that every man could make himself over in the image of success, if he would only determine to do so. Through willpower sloth could be transformed into industry, wastefulness into frugality, and intemperance into sobriety. "To the man of vigorous will, there are few impossibilities," said a clerical adviser. "Obstructions melt before his fiat like spring snowflakes."[13] It mattered little whether the obstructions consisted of defects of character or defects of circumstance, for a strong will could conquer all. "*Will* it, and it is thine," said a typical self-help handbook. "No longer grovel as though the hand of fate were upon thee. Stand erect. Thou art a man, and thy mission is a noble one."[14] The eternal boast of the self-made man was that he had overcome every limiting circumstance, and in so doing had won a higher station in life than fate had intended for him.

II

Of the cultivated qualities that helped men to rise, industry was the one most often prescribed and most elaborately justified by self-help advisers. The standard justification started with an assault on idleness, emphasizing at the outset that a lazy man forfeited his claim to humanity and violated all the higher requirements of his nature. According to William A. Alcott, a Connecticut schoolmaster, the idle man was scarcely human: "he is half quadruped, and of the most stupid species too."[15] Alcott could not conceive how a rational being could squander the precious gift of life through unproductive idleness. Nor could Andrew Carnegie conceive of such a course. When only a boy he revealed an appreciation of this commonplace of the success cult by confiding to his diary that labor was the universal law of life. Other experts, observing that many men sought relief from boredom through work, argued therefrom that idleness was repugnant to man's physical and spiritual nature. "To any healthy nature idleness is an intolerable burden," a clergyman declared, "and its enforced endurance a more painful penance than the hardest labors." [16]

The case against idleness also included the material argument that laziness doomed men to obscurity and failure. Franklin's Poor Richard was not the last to suggest that the sleeping fox catches no poultry, or that laziness travels so slowly that poverty soon overtakes him. For generation after generation Franklin's successors denounced indolence as the principal obstacle which blocked the road to fame and fortune. "More young men are hindered from arriving at positions of honor and usefulness, by indolence and want of order, than from any other causes," a typical handbook declared.[17]

Condemnation of idleness proceeded on social as well as personal grounds, for most authorities agreed that the well-being of society depended on the exertions of the individual. "To live in idleness, even if you have the means, is not only injurious to yourself, but a species of fraud upon the community," said William A. Alcott.[18] From society's point of view the idler could not justify his existence, for "He cannot engage himself in any employment or profession, because he will never have diligence enough to follow it; he can succeed in no undertaking, for he will never pursue it. He must be a bad husband, father, and relation, for he will not take the least pains to preserve his wife, children, and family from starving; and he must be a worthless friend, for he would not draw his hand from his bosom, though to prevent the destruction of the universe." [19] Was it any wonder that society condemned idlers to poverty and disgrace?

Nor was it any more surprising that those who commanded wealth and honor were the industrious men who had been trained to believe that energetic labor could accomplish anything. "Let those who would leave their mark in the world pull off their coats, roll up their sleeves, and set manfully to work," said one authority; ". . . hosts of successful men have risen from the humbler walks of life, brushing away, by industry and force of character, the social impediments to their upward flight, with which the peculiarity of their birth essayed to fetter them." [20] Since this was a lesson best learned in childhood, homilies on industry had a prominent place in school textbooks. The famous McGuffey readers, for example, extolled the glories of labor to several generations of American youth:

Work, work, my boy, be not afraid;
Look labor boldly in the face;
Take up the hammer or the spade,
And blush not for your humble place.

However poor or unfortunate, no boy had any reason to despair as long as he was willing to work. "Persevering industry will enable one to accomplish almost anything," said a New England common school textbook.

"It makes the smallest man equal to the greatest labors. By it Lilliputians can bind a Gulliver, or a mouse can release a lion from captivity." [21]

Successful businessmen frequently claimed that they owed everything to superior industry. When a Brooklyn clergyman questioned some five hundred prominent men in 1883, three out of four attributed their success to the work habits they cultivated in youth.[22] Russell Sage, writing for the Hearst syndicate in 1903, testified that he, like other prominent businessmen of his generation, so loved work he even despised holidays. "Work has been the chief, and, you might say, the only source of pleasure in my life," Sage asserted; "it has become the strongest habit that I have and the only habit that I would find it impossible to break." [23] When Frank W. Taussig and C. S. Joslyn questioned twentieth-century business leaders they discovered that many still attributed their triumphs to superior industry. Typical comments ran as follows:

> Just an average man, but I work at it harder than the average man.
>
> Hard knocks, hard work, long hours, and constant plugging produced results.
>
> Success comes from honesty and industry. . . . On the farm I learned to work and no matter how hard I had to work afterwards it was comparatively easy.
>
> I was brought up in a small town where I learned that work was the normal lot of man, not a misfortune, as is taught now.[24]

To what degree successful businessmen actually did work, or what the relation of industry actually was to success is almost impossible to determine. One can easily discount their own testimonies on the basis of bias, but it is more difficult to write off the observations of those whose personal careers were not concerned. Matthew H. Smith, a journalist who had firsthand knowledge of the failings and virtues of New York's post-Civil-War business leaders, reported that most of these men worked like galley slaves. Men like A. T. Stewart and William B. Astor, for example, put in more hours than any of their employees, and never sought relief from work except on Sunday. Foreign observers sometimes commented that this intense work psychology extended beyond the business community to include the entire nation. America seemed to be the only country where a man felt ashamed if he had nothing to do. In 1904 a British observer reported that in the American business community idling was not only despised but dull: there were no interesting men with whom to do nothing. The American man of affairs, he averred, took his work along with him to dinner, theater, and bed, and when he won success at last, he thought not of retiring, but of expanding his operations.[25] "Study the lives of successful men," said the self-made journalist, Edward Bok, "and the story will be found in each case exactly the same. The methods vary, as they must, but the actual basis of every successful life is the persistent, hard, hard work of years, and many a personal sacrifice." [26] After studying the careers of American millionaires Sorokin came to the same conclusion, for he believed it would have been difficult to find a busier, more energetic, harder-working group than America's leading moneymakers. However useful Thorstein Veblen's "conspicuous leisure" concept might be in describing the activities of the descendants of wealthy men, Sorokin thought it of little value in approaching the careers of the moneymakers themselves. Despite such expert testimony, the industry attributed to business leaders as a distinct group was undoubtedly overestimated; common sense suggests that no one trait could have been so generally characteristic. "Name me any manner of man you care to," said one thoughtful writer, "and I will name you a millionaire to correspond." [27] Precisely the same objection can be raised against the other virtues imputed to self-made men in order to explain their triumphs.

Perseverance followed close behind industry in the success cult's catalogue of virtues. The persevering man would not admit defeat or even discouragement, and fortunately so, for even the most optimistic self-help advisers admitted that in the upward climb he was bound to have to face both. It was only the man who would plod on, regardless of temporary setbacks, who could win the ultimate victory. "All that I have accomplished, or expect or hope to accomplish," said one self-made man, "has been or will be by that plodding, patient, persevering process of accretion which builds the ant-heap—particle by particle, thought by thought, fact by fact." [28] This was also a lesson of the McGuffey readers:

TRY, TRY AGAIN

If you find your task is hard
Try, try again;
Time will bring you your reward,
Try, try again;
All that other folks can do,
Why, with patience, should not you?
Only keep this rule in view:
Try, try again.

"Perseverance is the great thing," said John D. Rockefeller, in deducing the rules of success from his own career. "The young man who sticks is the one who succeeds." [29]

In the year 1786 Thomas Jefferson told a friend that he would welcome the appearance of any missionary who would make frugality the basis of his religious system, and who would go about the country preaching it as the only way to salvation. Had Jefferson lived into the last half of the nineteenth century he would have witnessed hundreds of such missionaries at work, preaching that very gospel. It was a poor success philosopher who did not urge young men to emulate the bee in storing up reserves against the winter of want. The art of making income exceed expenditures was hailed as one of the noblest private virtues, and a sure foundation for personal fortune. The man who husbanded his receipts, guarded against needless expenditures, and placed his savings at interest was certain to become a man of wealth. He who neglected this duty would suffer a reverse fortune. As Horace Greeley warned an audience of young men at the Cooper Union in 1867, the spendthrift was certain to "die a poor man, and, if he lives in this city, he will probably be buried at the public cost." [30] Beyond its importance to the security of private fortune frugality was also important to society as a whole. Capital was scarce in nineteenth-century America, and sorely needed for the development of railroads, factories, mines, and other vital industrial projects. The man who made it a practice to save money became a public benefactor in his ability to provide capital for such purposes. "Man must exercise thrift and save before he can produce anything material of great value," [31] Andrew Carnegie reasoned. Capitalists always sought saving young men as their partners, according to Carnegie, because savings offered proof that the beginner possessed the inner virtues necessary for the creation of capital.

In seeking partners or employees capitalists also looked for the quality of sobriety, if the gospel of success can be believed. Sobriety meant the total moral deportment of the young man, not just control of his drinking habits; and moral deportment was important because he who had no reputation allegedly had no credit. Drinking, smoking, and the keeping of late hours and fast company were all vigorously condemned by self-help theorists, for such practices cost heavily in time and money, and jeopardized the health and reputation of the practitioner.

One mid-nineteenth-century moralist estimated that the drinking man consumed twenty-five thousand dollars in a fifty-year period. No businessman could afford to squander his capital in this way. Bankers and financiers, men who professed to have firsthand knowledge in this field, were especially vehement in denouncing drink. In 1856 Wesley Smead, a Cincinnati banker, asserted that the liquor habit inevitably dragged a businessman down to failure: "It ruins his credit, wastes his property, destroys his health, and brings him to a premature grave." [32] Russell Sage, a more eminent financier, was equally convinced on this point. "I have never used any intoxicating liquor or wine of any kind in my long life," Sage declared in 1903, "and it is my honest belief that if it was not for that I should not have retained my health until now." [33] Tobacco suffered the same criticism. According to one estimate the habitual smoker puffed away eight thousand dollars in fifty years, while the "vile masticator of the filthy weed" chewed up five thousand over a similar period. Russell Sage attacked smoking as a terrible time-waster, pointing out that smokers usually enjoyed themselves best while reclining in easy chairs, a practice shunned by men intent upon success.

Toward the middle of the century success advisers also warned ambitious youth against the pleasures of bad company and the theater. Wealth did not come to those who wasted their time "on the pavements of Broadway, in ladies' drawing rooms, in cafes, and in theaters." [34] Arthur Tappan, the prominent New York merchant, forbade his employees to attend the theater, or even to associate with entertainers. Tappan may have had in mind the warning of William Van Doren, a New York clergyman, who called attention to the possible double meaning of the familiar theater sign ENTRANCE TO THE PIT. If the young businessman did not ruin his prospects by theater-going, he certainly did not improve them either. "The fast young man, who with his sweet-heart, visits the theatre on the average of three times a week, spends in fifty years a fortune of near $50,000," declared one moralist who had an interest in the money cost of this vice; [35] the moral cost, of course, was incalculable.

Thanks to the relaxation of moral standards in the urban centers, and to the growth of big businesses in which it was impossible for the employer to supervise the morals of all his employees, prohibitions against drinking, smoking, and theater-going did not survive the century. In 1885 when Andrew Carnegie warned a group of business college students against drunkenness and the frequenting of bars he insisted that he was no temperance lecturer in disguise. To prove his point he told his audience that a drink at mealtime would not adversely affect their business careers. Carnegie and others emphasized moderation rather than abstinence. "I do not preach total abstinence of any habits to which human nature is prone," said Edward Bok. "Every man ought to know what is good for him and what is injurious to his best interests. But an excess of anything is injurious, and a young man on the threshold of a business career cannot afford to be excessive in a single direction." [36] Any pleasure was dangerous if it befuddled the mind or fatigued the body, making it unfit for the work of the morrow. The responsible young man was the one who knew that his obligations to his employer extended through his off-duty hours as well as through his working day.

III

When a young man had mastered these major virtues he had taken a long step forward on the path to success. But the road was long and the obstacles many; he would need other virtues to sustain him along the way. Above all he would need to develop those qualities which most impressed employers. Since the employee who came to work on time was the one who caught his master's eye, the cultivation of habits of punctuality became a prime necessity. "Holding punctuality among the major virtues, he is ever true to the appointed hour," said Horace Mann, "and as he goes and comes, men set their watches by him, as though he were a clock-face of the sun, and moved by solar machinery." [37] According to experts on success this robotlike quality always impressed employers, and always won rewards.

The wise employee would also strive to be both reliable and indispensable. "Let your eye light up at his request, and your feet be nimble," said one guide to wealth; "be the arch upon which your employer may rest with safety; let him feel that he may intrust you with uncounted gold." [38] At all times an employee who wished to get ahead placed his employer's interests above his own. "Eliminate your personal self," one authority advised, "endeavor to become to your employer a thoughtful machine, and the meed of respect and confidence that will be yours will amply compensate." [39] Naturally, the youth who thought first of his employer's interest would not run off and leave him when superior opportunities beckoned. Instead he followed the example of the wise young man of the McGuffey reader who testified that "When I had a good place and was getting on well, I was not willing to leave it and spend some days or weeks in trying to find a better place. When other young men said, 'Come with us, and we will find you something better to do,' I shook my head, and stuck to my bush. After a while my employers took me into partnership with them in their business." [40] Too often the desire for a new job was born of the deluded idea that other men worked under better conditions. The sensible man never wavered in his loyalties. "Remember, you have passed through espousals, and are new wedded," said a clergyman who favored sticking it out in one job. "Preserve your chastity with it; and when you are blessed with its profits and joys, welcome them as a legitimate posterity." [41]

Nor did the correct employee ever disobey his master's commands. As long as the employer required no dishonorable service, every command, no matter how personally repugnant, was to be cheerfully fulfilled. "Be willing to undertake whatever task is assigned to you, pleasant or not," a speaker told an audience of young men at Chautauqua in 1892. "If it comes in the regular course of duty . . . don't hesitate, step right up and go through with it." [42] Employees were paid to obey, not to command. "Let a young man in business show that he is capable of carrying out the wishes of his employer," said Edward Bok, "and he demonstrates a most valuable quality. To do a thing precisely as one is told to do it is the first step to success." [43] "Always obey instructions," John D. Rockefeller advised; "you must learn to obey orders before you can hope to give them." [44]

Not only must an employee cheerfully accept the tasks required of him, he must also be sure to execute each and every one, giving particular attention to little details. A trail of half-done or badly done jobs never led to success. "Many a man acquires a fortune by doing his business thoroughly," said P. T. Barnum, "while his neighbor remains poor for life, because he only half does it." [45] "It is the surest key to success in business," Edward Bok declared, "thoroughness in everything a man does; thoroughness, especially in little things." [46]

The valuable employee also demonstrated initiative. This was an especially useful virtue in the years following 1890, when corporate arrangements made it impossible for owners to know and direct the work of their employees. "Spare no effort to get acquainted with the entire business," said one adviser, "bearing in mind the important but often overlooked fact that men who can enlarge their employer's interests . . . are always more valuable than those who simply . . . follow the same dull routine year after year without progressing as the world moves forward." [47] The employee who merely filled his position deserved but a small payment; the man who knew how to do more than was required of him, however, was a man of executive genius who could expect commensurate reward. In large businesses underlings were especially fortunate in that they often knew more about their specialized departments than owners could possibly know, and thus had greater opportunities to act independently and beyond the exact requirements of their jobs. This was the fact behind Andrew Carnegie's rule that employees should break orders to save owners.

According to the rules of the game no special recognition or pay should be expected for extra services; appreciation for initiative should be taken for granted. "This is where so many young people make a fatal mistake," said Orison Marden, "in begrudging over-services which they render and for which they get no recognition or pay." [48] It was only the man who earned more than he was paid who was worthy of the advancements that were sure to come. President Charles R. Van Hise of the University of Wisconsin warned the university's graduating class of 1907 to remember that if they wished for success "Each of you should appreciate that the only possible way in which promotion can come to you is by earning more than you are receiving. . . . No other basis will be recognized. All who are worthy of the places they occupy, whether janitors or heads of divisions, are earning more than they are receiving. These only may hope for advancement." [49] Charles M. Schwab had the same thought in mind when he advised employees not to be afraid of imperiling their health by working extra hours for the company that paid their salary. The man who counted his hours and complained about his pay was destined to be a self-elected failure. "If more persons would get so enthused over their day's

work that some one would have to remind them to go out to lunch there would be more happiness in the world and less indigestion," Schwab proclaimed. "If you must be a glutton, be a glutton for work." [50]

Behind all these exhortations to economic virtue lay the idea that the drama of economic salvation paralleled that of spiritual salvation in every particular. The god of the business universe was the employer, who, like the true deity, was just, providing for all a way unto salvation. Those who willed salvation and diligently cultivated industry, frugality, sobriety, perseverance, punctuality, loyalty, obedience, initiative, and a host of kindred virtues, would find their reward in success. Those who willed damnation on the other hand and cultivated the virtues conducive thereto, would sin their way to economic hell. The employer-god knew the ways of the just and the unjust; no secret could be hid from his prying eye, for "Employers are not blind to what is going on around them, and though they may often seem unobservant, they are always watching those under them. They know who shirks, who watches the clock, who clips a few minutes here and there from his employer's time, who comes a little late in the morning and goes a little earlier in the evening; in other words, they keep thoroughly posted in regard to the work and general conduct of their employees." [51] The employer-god recorded the sins and good works of every man in his book of judgment and on the day of reckoning knew who deserved poverty and who wealth. Among the damned many cried out against poverty's torments, but in their hearts they knew they had earned their fate.

God and Mammon

IV

MATTHEW H. SMITH, who had a double career as a clergyman and a Wall Street journalist, spoke wisely in the year 1878 when he predicted that whoever wrote the history of American business would also have to write the history of religion. Having served both God and Mammon, Smith was conscious of their relationship and sensed that justice could not be done to one if the other were ignored. As it turned out, European not American investigators first explored the connection between capitalism and Protestantism. Thanks to Max Weber, Ernst Troeltsch, Richard Tawney and others, the complex relation of religion to the spirit of business enterprise has been carefully and critically examined. Thanks also to fruitless debates on whether Protestantism caused capitalism, or *vice versa,* the fact of their historic congeniality has too often been lost to view.[1]

In nineteenth-century America religion and business were no less partners in common enterprise than they had been in seventeenth-century England. Both Weber and Tawney erred in assuming that in the eighteenth century religious and moral foundations of the get-ahead gospel had been swept away by secular currents. Weber, for example, looked upon Benjamin Franklin as a classic symbol of the secularization of the Protestant ethic, an ethic "without the religious basis, which by Franklin's time had died away." [2] Tawney contended that by the nineteenth century the church possessed no independent standards to which economic practice was expected to conform, and that the church's customary warnings against materialism "wore more and more the air of afterthoughts." [3] If this means that Russell Conwell had less power to enforce fair business practices in Philadelphia than John Calvin had in Geneva, the point must be conceded without debate. But if it means that Conwell and his clerical associates had no serious interest in the morality of success, and had nothing to teach in this sphere, the contention must be emphatically denied. Throughout the nineteenth century religious and moral precepts provided the foundation for the self-help creed, and clergymen who preached the gospel of success encouraged their business allies to behave in a conscionable manner. Their counsel was often ignored, but the fact of failure should not obscure the extent and vigor of the effort.

One of the impressive facts about the American cult of self-help is that many of its leading proponents were clergymen. The names of Henry Ward Beecher, Lyman Abbott, William Lawrence, Russell Conwell, and Horatio Alger were as familiar to readers of success tracts as to those who worshipped in the leading Protestant churches on the Sabbath. By teaching that godliness was in league with riches such spokesmen put the sanction of the church on the get-ahead values of the business community. And by so teaching they encouraged each rising generation to believe that it was possible to serve both God and Mammon.

Like the businessmen whose careers they glorified, these clergy were of the Protestant faith. Fully 90 percent of the leading American businessmen of the early twentieth century were Protestant, and of the well-known clergy who pointed the way to wealth, none was a Roman Catholic.[4] Despite Catholicism's numerical strength in the urban centers where the great fortunes were made, no eminent prelate wrote books or preached sermons urging young men to seek salvation along the road to wealth. The reasons for this negative performance are obvious. Since there were relatively few Catholics in the American business elite, probably never more than 7 percent prior to 1900, the Church had no special interest in glorifying this group. Furthermore, less than 10 percent of the nation's business leaders were foreign born. In ministering to immigrants in the years after the Civil War, and especially to those from southern and eastern Europe, the Catholic Church was working with men who had very little chance of achieving outstanding financial success.[5] In addition, by standing aloof from the glorification of wealth, Catholic spokesmen upheld their church's traditional indictment of materialism.

Virtually all the leading Protestant denominations, with the exception of the Lutheran, produced at least one nationally known clergyman who honored the wealth-through-virtue theme.[6] Most of these ministers, like the business leaders of the time, were natives of the New England and the Middle Atlantic states. Almost without exception they had pulpits in the financial and industrial centers of the North and East, and by virtue of their location, and the economic status of their congregations, they had easy contact with businessmen and business values. A substantial number were Calvinists: the Congregational church produced more prominent self-help publicists than any other denomination. How much this was due to theology, and how much to the church's dominant position in industrial New England no one can say, but there is a suggestion in the fact that rural clergymen did little to glorify the cult of self-help, while their urban brethren, Calvinists and non-Calvinists alike, preached it as true gospel.

Consider some of the nineteenth-century Congregational clergy who, by their utterances on success, proved themselves worthy successors to Cotton Mather. One of the earliest of these was John Todd, who lectured on *The Foundations of Success* in 1843, and subsequently wrote two self-help handbooks, *The Young Man* (1845) and *Nuts for Boys to Crack* (1866). Todd was no back-country preacher, though his pulpit was at Pittsfield, Massachusetts, in the extreme western portion of the state. The fact that Todd preached at Pittsfield when it was developing as an important shoe and textile manufacturing center probably had something to do with his interest in worldly success. Matthew H. Smith began his career as a Congregational clergyman in 1842 at Malden, Massachusetts, a boot and shoe center not far removed from Boston. After eight years in Malden Smith moved to New York where he began a new career as a Wall Street journalist. In addition to his address, *The Elements of Success* (1854), Smith wrote *Twenty Years Among the Bulls and Bears of Wall Street* (1870), and *Successful Folks* (1878). Francis E. Clark, nationally famous as the founder of the Christian Endeavor Society, was a Congregational minister in Portland, Maine, the commercial metropolis of that state. His two self-help books, *Our Business Boys* (1884), and *Danger Signals, the Enemies of Youth from the Business Man's Standpoint* (1885), were based on ideas and information provided by Portland businessmen. Wilbur F. Crafts, who published *Successful Men of Today and What They Say of Success* (1883), occupied a pulpit in New Bedford, Massachusetts, a cotton manufacturing center, before moving to larger pastorates in Chicago and Brooklyn. Through *Seven Lectures to Young Men* (1844) Henry Ward Beecher had established himself as an expert on self-help long before he began to preach industry, frugality, and sobriety to the wealthy congregation of Brooklyn's Plymouth Church. Lyman Abbott followed in Beecher's footsteps, taking over the pastorate of Plymouth Church in 1887. His book, *How to Succeed* (1882), established him as a true prophet of the success cult.

Though Congregational ministers were most prominent in this line they had considerable competition from leaders of other faiths. The principal Episcopal self-help spokesman was William Lawrence, Bishop of Massachusetts and son of the industrialist Amos A. Lawrence. He memorialized success values in his *Life of Amos A. Lawrence* (1888) and in a famous essay on the "Relation of Wealth to Morals," published in *The World's Work* in 1901.[7] William Van Doren, author of *Mercantile Morals* (1852) occupied a pulpit of the Dutch Reformed Church at Piermont, New York, the town that served as the first eastern terminus of the Erie Railroad. The leading Baptist spokesman was Russell Conwell, a self-made Yankee who built the Baptist Temple in Philadelphia, founded Temple University, and created a popular sensation with his success sermon, *Acres of Diamonds*. Methodism was represented by Daniel Wise, a one-time grocer's apprentice who filled many pulpits in the commercial and industrial towns of New England and New Jersey, and glorified the self-made man in his book, *Uncrowned Kings* (1875).

Of all the popularizers of self-help values none was better known to the post–Civil-War generation than Horatio Alger, who got his start as a Unitarian minister at Brewster, Massachusetts, in 1864. Like Matthew H. Smith before him, Alger abandoned both the pulpit and New England for a literary career in New York. He found his inspirations in the city, as did others who played upon the rags-to-riches theme. Unlike Smith, who reported the doings of Wall Street operators, Alger concentrated on boys who had not yet arrived. He invested his heroes with all the moral virtues honored by the cult of self-help, but even in this he was different, in that Ragged Dick and Tattered Tom won success by some sudden stroke, rather than by steady application to business. These features, together with his preference for the fictional form, set Alger apart from other leading writers in this field.[8]

Even without Alger the success-minded clergy represented a numerous host, and one of great influence in the cult of self-help. They wrote many of the books of its bible, preached its gospel, tried to restrain its excesses, and protected it against the charge of godlessness and materialism. In nineteenth-century America, where the mass of men respected business and religion, the partnership organized by the clergy proved profitable to both.

II

The doctrine of the secular calling provided the foundation for the religious defense of worldly success. In proclaiming this doctrine American clergymen, like their European predecessors, argued that God required every man to lead a successful and useful temporal life as well as an acceptable spiritual life. Under this conception the calling was an exacting worldly enterprise in which man could conquer his own base nature and overcome the limitations of his social environment. The man who succeeded in his vocation proved that he deserved a high station in this life as well as salvation in the next. Since every man won salvation in his profession, and not outside it, God provided a suitable calling for all. As one authority explained, "The principle is, that however poor, ignorant, or prone to evil we are born, God gives to each a glorious opportunity. If true to him, and if rightly alive to our great advantages, we may make our fortune." [9]

Throughout the nineteenth century clergymen and laymen alike insisted that business stood high on God's list of approved callings. Matthew H. Smith, writing for *Hunt's Merchants' Magazine* in 1854, asserted that God had ordained business as the great purpose in life. "The race were [*sic*] made for employment," Smith said. "Adam was created and placed in the Garden of Eden for business purposes; it would have been better for the race if he had attended closely to the occupation for which he was made." [10] The man who chose business as a career did not have to fear that he would be cut off from opportunities for spiritual improvement, for the spiritual and the material were united in business. Theodore Parker emphasized this point when he described the merchant as "a moral educator, a church of Christ gone into business—a saint in trade . . . the Saint of the nineteenth century is the Good Merchant; he is wisdom for the foolish, strength for the weak, warning to the wicked, and a blessing to all. Build him a shrine in Bank and Church, in the Market and the Exchange . . .

no Saint stands higher than this Saint of Trade." [11] Despite the secularization of American thought in the latter part of the century, the theme of the God-appointed business calling did not lose its popularity with either clerical or lay writers. As the century closed, Orison Marden warned his readers against the "fatal error" of regarding the church as sacred and the warehouse as secular, for both were sacred and uplifting. In the year 1898, Charles P. Masden, a Methodist clergyman in Milwaukee, told a group of business college students that business was not just an occupation but a divine calling. "It is sacred," Masden declared. "It is a means of grace. It is a stewardship. It is building up for eternity, and laying up treasures in heaven." [12]

This did not mean that God disapproved the laying up of treasures on earth. Far from it, for in the American cult of success, as in the Calvinist ethic, the pursuit of wealth became a positive religious duty. Reverend Thomas P. Hunt, one of the earliest writers on this subject, summarized the case for riches in the title of his work: *The Book of Wealth; in Which It Is Proved from the Bible that It Is the Duty of Every Man to Become Rich* (1836). Lyman Abbott rejoiced in the parable of the talents, and used it to justify his claim that Jesus approved the building of great fortunes. "He did not condemn wealth," Abbott declared. "On the contrary, he approved of the use of accumulated wealth to accumulate more wealth." [13] Russell Conwell agreed, for in *Acres of Diamonds* he asserted that it was man's "Christian and godly duty" to seek wealth. Secular writers were especially pleased to have such friendly assurances from the clergy. Edwin T. Freedley, for one, argued that as long as religion sanctioned accumulation, no other sanction was needed.

If religion blessed business by approving the pursuit of wealth it doubled the blessing by sanctifying all the economic virtues essential to its accumulation. Of the virtues dear to the business community, religion exalted industry above all others. God required hard, continuous labor of rich and poor alike, not only as punishment for original sin, but as a constructive means of personal discipline. Labor kept man from sensuality, intemperance, and moral degeneration. It offered an opportunity to worship and glorify God through imitation of his creative labors. When combined with other virtues it allowed man to lay up treasures on earth as well as in heaven, and helped him win an earthly success which served as a measure of his heavenly salvation. Protestant clergy of all denominations agreed that labor had special honor in the sight of God, and that it formed an integral part of true religion. Daniel Wise, a Methodist minister, spoke for all religious prophets of success when he advised a group of young men that "Religion will teach you that industry is a SOLEMN DUTY you owe to God, whose command is, 'BE DILIGENT IN BUSINESS!' "[14] The religious aspect of labor was emphasized so much in the nineteenth century that even secular-minded men sometimes talked of labor in religious terms. Andrew Carnegie, for example, once remarked that an honest day's work was "not a bad sort of prayer."[15]

Frugality also had special honor in the sight of God, and was considered like labor, a positive religious duty. In the tradition of the Protestant ethic the man who aspired to success and salvation was supposed to live simply and frugally, avoiding luxury and ostentation. This tradition carried over into the American ethic of self-help, whose clerical prophets advertised frugality as "the good genius whose presence guides the footsteps of every prosperous and successful man." [16] Through frugality God provided a way to wealth which was open to all, and one which all were supposed to travel. The great exemplar of frugality was none other than Jesus of Nazareth, who, after he had fed the multitude with loaves and fishes "commanded his disciples to gather up the fragments, lest anything should be wasted." [17] Frugality led inevitably to sobriety, for the man who husbanded his means had nothing left to spend on the vices. "Drinking habits," Henry Ward Beecher observed, "take hold indirectly upon the whole framework of a man's prosperity. They lead to very many expenses besides the daily expenses of the cup." [18]

According to the theology of success God always rewarded the industrious, the frugal, and the sober with wealth. One Episcopal clergyman argued that it would have been surprising indeed if God had not provided material rewards for the faithful practice of his appointed virtues. These rewards, said the cleric, "like all the profit of godliness, are to be gathered in this life as well as in that which is to come." [19] According to this logic the possession of wealth made the possessor one of the elect. Wealth was a gift from God, an evidence of his favor, and a reward for faithfulness—comforting doctrine to substantial pew-holders in urban churches. Apologists who turned to the Scriptures noted that Abraham, Solomon and other Old Testament heroes received wealth from the Lord in token of his approval. "The Old Testament doctrine of wealth is frank and unmistakable," a Unitarian minister told his congregation in 1885. "It is a *blessing from the Lord.* It is a sign of the divine approval. . . ."[20] Little wonder, in view of such assurances, that John D. Rockefeller brushed off his critics with the simple assertion that it was God who had given him his money.

In accounting for the superior prosperity of the well-to-do, clergymen invariably pointed to their superior morality. Russell Conwell insisted that ninety-eight out of every hundred rich Americans stood above their fellowmen in honesty. "That is why they are rich," he said. "That is why they are trusted with money. That is why they carry on great enterprises and find plenty of people to work with them. It is because they are honest men."[21] If one were to accept the gospel of success at face value he would believe that virtually every rich man was a paragon of moral virtue. William Lawrence, Episcopal Bishop of Massachusetts, summarized the clerical point of view when he observed that "in the long run, it is only to the man of morality that wealth comes. . . . We, like the Psalmist, occasionally see the wicked prosper, but only occasionally. . . . Godliness is in league with riches."[22]

Turned around, this doctrine meant that wickedness was in league with poverty. Those who were poor had no reason to reproach the Giver of Gifts, for they had been tested and found deficient in virtue. "It is no respect for persons that causes the Lord to make some rich and some poor," said one authority, "but it comes of His infinite love to all, and His effort to save all from the evils and corruptions of their own hearts."[23] The man who complained against God's wise way of distributing wealth had the root of evil in him. "And is the young man aware, when repining at his penury, that he is reproaching his Maker, and charging Him indirectly with being stingy?" another clergyman asked.[24]

By identifying the rich with the elect and the poor with the damned, clergymen provided strong religious and moral defenses for the well-to-do. He who attacked the rich, or urged a system of distribution favorable to the poor, automatically advertised himself as an enemy of God and of the moral order. Thanks to the religious defense of money-making, wealthy Americans of the nineteenth century knew the meaning of the assurance offered by one popular success handbook: "Heaven taketh notes of thy career, and the angels are guardian watchers and abettors of thy prosperity." [25]

III

No one-way system of advantages characterized the partnership of God and Mammon. In return for the sanction of religion, businessmen were supposed to be sincerely religious, identifying themselves with the doctrines and activities of the church. Clergymen and laymen alike agreed that the way to wealth passed through the church. A Methodist minister, Daniel Wise, insisted that the qualities necessary for success appeared most often in those who embraced and faithfully followed the teachings of Christ. And William Speer, a lay writer, claimed it was more important for the young man to begin his business career with proper religious perceptions than with a diploma "certifying that he is master of all the 'ologies' of all the colleges." [26] Since Bible-reading developed proper religious perceptions, businessmen were constantly advised to seek inspiration in the Scriptures, especially in Solomon's Proverbs. By the same token they were supposed to shun those intellectual influences which undermined faith. In the 1890s, after Darwinism, the higher criticism, and the social gospel had made inroads on traditional religion, Edward Bok warned prospective businessmen that one of the keys to success was strict adherence to the ancient creeds. The man who rejected the faith of his fathers invited disaster. "Without that faith, without that absolute conviction," Bok declared, "he will be hindered and crippled in whatever he undertakes." [27] Except for Andrew Carnegie, the major post–Civil-War titans did not cripple themselves by straying off the paths of orthodoxy. And at the turn of the twentieth century the vast majority of American business leaders still identified themselves with the Episcopal, Presbyterian, Methodist, Baptist, and other respectable Protestant churches.

Mere affiliation was not enough, however. The responsible man of affairs attended church regularly, after the manner of J. P. Morgan, Jay Cooke, John D. Rockefeller, Peter Cooper, and a host of others. Even on weekdays periods of formal worship had their uses. J. P. Morgan sometimes left his office in mid-afternoon to go to St. George's Church, to pray and sing hymns, hour after hour. In the years after the Civil War, Wall Street capitalists paused on their way to the Exchange to seek the Lord's blessing in Trinity Church or stopped there at the end of the day to offer thanks for victories won. Nearby, at the old Dutch church, every day many of the most prominent men on the Street dropped their worldly cares at noon to commune with God through prayer.[28] These worshippers probably agreed with another famous churchgoer, Daniel Drew, who observed that "When a man goes to prayer meeting and class meeting two nights of the week, and to church twice on Sunday, and on week days works at his office from morning till night, his life is made up of about two things—work and worship." [29]

Sometimes these men also played an active role in the work of the church. In addition to attending Episcopal conventions as a deputy from New York, J. P. Morgan usually transported the leading church dignitaries to the convention city. Peter Cooper fulfilled his obligations to the Lord by serving as a Sunday School superintendent, while John D. Rockefeller taught industry, frugality, and sobriety to young men in a Baptist Bible class. Nor were these exceptional cases. Two close observers of the New York business community testified that the most prominent merchants and financiers could usually be found on Sabbath mornings in the churches interpreting the Scriptures.[30] Making money was important but saving souls appeared to go along with it hand in hand.

If a man had no talents as an evangelist he could at least pay the way for those who did. Men of wealth were expected to support the local work of the church and to underwrite missionary activity in distant vineyards. Methodist ministers encouraged Daniel Drew to endow a theological seminary which would send men out to preach the gospel to a sinful world. The more common tactic was to ask for more magnificent houses of worship; the Astors, Vanderbilts, Rockefellers, Wanamakers, Morgans, Armours, Pullmans, and Mellons were all builders of churches.

Even in the conduct of business affairs there were opportunities to promote religion. In hiring clerks employers could give preference to those with religious connections; self-interest suggested such a policy anyway. They might also coerce clerks into participating in religious observances. Arthur Tappan was exceptional, no doubt, but he showed what could be done. Tappan required his clerks to attend prayer meetings twice a week and regular services twice on Sunday. Every Monday morning his employees had to report what church they had attended, the name of the clergyman, and the texts used as the basis of the sermon.[31] Those employers who had no desire to police the religious activities of their employees could still promote religion by not requiring them to work on the Sabbath and by not asking them to perform deeds that violated their religious scruples. The wise businessman respected evidence of Christian living at all times. "Don't scoff at those . . . who are trying to lead Christian lives," one adviser warned, "and don't for a moment belittle the importance of their competition in the struggle for supremacy. The quiet, easy, smooth-spoken man who is looked upon as a milk-sop, may have in him all the elements of business success." [32] William Van Doren, a Dutch Reformed minister, claimed that he knew one hard-hearted employer who rescinded a Sabbath working order when he discovered that his clerk was ready to sacrifice his job rather than violate the Lord's day. The employer "cared neither for God, heaven, hell, or worse, but he did care for a trusty clerk," Van Doren said. "He knew not the value of an interest in the Redeemer, but he did most accurately understand the value of one, whom nothing of pecuniary interest could tempt." [33] The clerk who advertised that he had lost his job by refusing to work on the Sabbath was bound to receive many offers of employment, for according to the cult of success, church-attending employers always sought Sabbath-observing employees. Creditors also took notice of who went to church. This led one success tract to advise that "A good advertisement for a working man, is a seat in church." [34]

By attending church, participating in its work, underwriting its expenses, and honoring its teachings, the businessman put his stamp of approval on religion. In so doing he reciprocated the application of religious sanctions to business, and sealed the partnership of God and Mammon.

IV

The application of these religious sanctions, however, was by no means automatic. Clergymen who identified themselves with the success cult did not hesitate to pass moral judgment on men and methods in business. Like other authorities on self-help they did not attempt to glorify notorious men like Jay Gould, Jim Fisk, or Daniel Drew, for they generally held that "No amount of money can make a highway robber or any other kind successful. . . . Even millions of plunder does not constitute success, which must include a good name." [35] P. T. Barnum was denounced by Matthew H. Smith who claimed that in his race for wealth Barnum had operated on the principle that any tactic was legitimate so long as it was not criminal. "Humbug, tricks, deceit, low cunning, false stories, were stock in trade," Smith declared.[36] And Henry Ward Beecher pointed from his Plymouth pulpit to "an old obese abomination of money" operating in Wall Street, and warned his congregation against worshipping such a man. "He has utterly defiled and destroyed his manhood in the manufacturing of wealth," Beecher charged; "he is a great epitomized, circulating hell on earth, and when he dies, hell will groan —one more woe." [37]

In order to enjoy the approval of the church wealth had to be earned in an honorable calling, one that contributed to the social welfare. Saloon-keepers, speculators, gamblers, and others who rendered no useful service could not qualify. Merchants, manufacturers, and bankers were honored by the clergy as long as they kept in touch with the needs of mankind and provided the necessary capital, goods, and services. "When will you manufacturers learn that you must know the changing needs of humanity if you would succeed in life?" Russell Conwell asked. "Apply yourselves, all you Christian people, as manufacturers or merchants or workmen to supply that human need. It is a great principle as broad as humanity and as deep as the Scripture itself." [38]

The clergy knew that an honorable calling was not enough, however, for there were many dishonorable men in reputable vocations. Too many businessmen agreed with the sentiment attributed to Daniel Drew. "A business man has got to get along somehow," he said. "Better that my hog should come dirty home, than no hog at all." [39] Such men, even if they acquired wealth, did not have any honor among clerical writers of success tracts. "Riches got by fraud, are dug out of one's own heart and destroy the mine," said Henry Ward Beecher. "Unjust riches curse the owner in getting, in keeping, in transmitting." [40] William Van Doren, who was aware of the questionable tactics of many New York businessmen, insisted that in all fortunes dishonestly acquired there was a curse which "sooner or later will break forth like a leprosy." [41] To a widespread belief in the business community that the completely honest man was at a disadvantage in the quest for wealth, the clergy answered that whatever the short-term disadvantages, honesty brought the long-term gains. Though the wicked might enjoy a temporary prosperity, the laws of moral retribution would deprive them of permanent fortune.

Ministers constantly warned moneymakers of the moral dangers inherent in their quest. These warnings were not inspired by religious objections to wealth, but rather by the fear that the passion for money would lead men into sin. The only man who could seek wealth and remain morally upright was the one who was capable of the most rigorous personal discipline. "If you have entered this shining way, begin to look for snares and traps," warned Henry Ward Beecher. "Go not careless of your danger, and provoking it." While one rich man climbed into heaven, ten sank into the bottomless pit of hell. "You seek a land pleasant to the sight, but dangerous to the feet," Beecher declared, "a land of fragrant winds, which lull to security; of golden fruits, which are poisonous; of glorious hues, which dazzle and mislead." [42]

All wealth-seekers ran the risk of making accumulation an end in itself. Religion warned her business partner against this deadly sin. "It is folly supreme, nay madness," said William Van Doren, "to make the acquiring riches, and enjoying them, the chief end of life." [43] The man who coveted wealth for its own sake was a mere beast of burden, who would go "toiling beneath his load, with gold on his back, and hell in his heart, down to destruction." [44] Clergymen who taught that Jesus approved the quest for wealth also taught that Jesus scorned the man who loved the quest for its own sake. He who did not think beyond the problems of accumulation was hell-bent. "The man that worships the dollar instead of thinking of the purposes for which it ought to be used, the man who idolizes simply money, the miser that hordes his money in the cellar, or hides it in his stocking, or refuses to invest it where it will do the world good, that man who hugs the dollar until the eagle squeals," Russell Conwell warned, "has in him the root of all evil." [45]

Since the twin of miserliness was prodigality, clergymen had to remind their business associates that God had not given them wealth just to live merrily and without care. In the eyes of the church it was a sin for the wealthy to waste their substance on luxurious clothing, lavish entertainment, great mansions, and other forms of ostentatious display. The rich man was meant to live simply and frugally, spending no more than necessary for his subsistence. Here, as elsewhere, moderation should characterize his actions; he should be neither miserly nor prodigal but follow instead a middle course.

The doctrine of the stewardship of wealth provided the clue to the right use of wealth. Since it was God who had made the rich man's lot different from that of his poor brother, his money was simply held in trust to be used in doing God's work. Thus it could not be used exclusively for his own benefit, but must be applied primarily to the benefit of others. In practice this meant support of schools, libraries, museums, orphanages, hospitals, churches, and similar beneficent institutions. As a onetime Unitarian minister, Ralph Waldo Emerson, explained, "They should own who can administer, not they who hoard and conceal; not they who, the great proprietors they are, are only the great beggars, but they whose work carves out the work for more, opens a path for all. For he is the rich man in whom the people are rich, and he is the poor man in whom the people are poor. . . ." [46] By this reasoning the good steward could be considered as much a saint as any saint of the church and as deserving of religious honor.

The church's teachings on the subject of wealth provided the foundation on which secular writers built an elaborate body of doctrine concerning the ethics of success, but they also provided the businessman with a convenient rationale by which he could justify his superior position in society. It would be a mistake, however, to assume that all those who used the rationale either lived by its precepts or gave them a respectful hearing. Occasionally God and Mammon exchanged harsh words. In 1891 an English Methodist minister, Hugh Price Hughes, condemned Andrew Carnegie for piling up a fortune at the expense of his fellowmen. Carnegie, who never took the partnership of business and religion seriously, was so nettled by the attack that he hurled back into the minister's teeth the parable of the talents and the teaching of John Wesley, founder of the Methodist faith: "Gain all you can by honest industry." [47] Clergymen, in time, grew weary of businessmen who quoted the Scriptures to suit their own purposes. It was no accident that the Episcopal and Congregational churches, which had led all others in providing spokesmen for the self-help cult before 1890, became the most productive of clergymen of the social gospel after that date. With the rise of the social gospel, ministers like Washington Gladden, George D. Herron, W. D. P. Bliss, Bouck White, and Walter Rauschenbusch tried to dissolve the partnership of God and Mammon.

The Way of the Just

V

WHATEVER ITS DEFECTS, no fair-minded critic can charge that the American gospel of success encouraged men to rise in the world by foul means as well as fair or to be indifferent to social welfare in the process. Priests of the cult did not proclaim

The simple rule, the good old plan,
That he should take who has the might,
And he shall keep who can.

A few robber barons may have been guided by this principle, but those who preached the gospel of self-help presented no such brief. Just as the immoralities of professing Christians provide no clue to the moral teachings of Christianity, so the antisocial behavior of a few notorious barons provides no accurate guide to the social teachings of the success creed. If critics charge Jay Gould, Jim Fisk, and Daniel Drew against the gospel of self-help, they must also add to its credit more responsible operators such as George Peabody, Peter Cooper, Ezra Cornell, and Andrew Carnegie, for it was the latter, not the former, who were acknowledged as the heroes of the cult.

So far as the literature of success reveals anything, it reveals that business apologists and business critics agreed that the man of affairs had far-reaching social responsibilities. They also agreed on the specific nature of those responsibilities and, in many instances, on the details of the corrupt businessman's sins against society. They did not agree, however, on the ways and means by which the required responsibility could be developed and the community protected against the crimes and excesses of those who lusted after gold. Critics of business insisted that these problems could not be solved without the aid of regulatory legislation and the active intervention of the state in economic affairs. Defenders of business, on the other hand, clung to the idea that good intentions, good private character, and the universal laws of moral retribution provided sufficient protection. Over against good laws, they proposed good men. The crime of the success apologist was not that he disregarded the question of public welfare, but rather that he was unbelievably naïve in his conviction that the educated conscience was capable of protecting and promoting the welfare of all. That belief, neatly summarized by Timothy S. Arthur in 1848, has served as the cornerstone of the success cult's social faith. "The common good," he said, "ought to be regarded by every man, and whoever seeks to secure the common good most effectively secures his own. This does not mean that a man should throw all his earnings into the treasury of the commonwealth, or do any act of similar kind; or that he should neglect his own interest in seeking to forward the interests of others. The arrangement of society, under the direction of an all-wise Providence, provides for every man's well-being in the pursuit of some employment that benefits the whole; and the conducting of those employments on right principles is nothing more than each man attending diligently to his own business in life, but without in any way interfering with his neighbor's business, or taking the slightest advantage of him in any mutual transactions. If such were the acknowledged laws of trade, the well-being of all would be secured." [1] In the hope of making such principles the acknowledged laws of trade self-help advisers attempted to awaken the social consciences of young men called to the quest for wealth.

Taking their cue from the clergy, secular authorities advised beginners that the business in which they chose to make their way must be one which enjoyed social approval by reason of its usefulness. Too many young men drifted into degrading businesses which elevated nobody and fulfilled no human need. If, by chance, fortune came their way, they could not justify it before mankind. It was not enough that money be gained without injury to the community; a fortune was supposed to stand as a measure of its possessor's service to the community. The capitalist who provided money for new enterprises had no reason to be ashamed of his wealth, nor did the manufacturer who produced quality goods and sold them at a low price or the merchant whose small profit margins allowed him to serve the maximum number of customers. "This may not be the popular judgment now," said Freeman Hunt in 1856, "but must one day become so, for Mankind is slowly learning to judge by the natural Law published by Jesus—that he who would be greatest of all, must be most effectively the Servant of all." [2]

In keeping with this conception the success cult taught that the speculator deserved nothing but condemnation. A distinction had to be drawn between the investor and the speculator, because the former supplied capital for legitimate enterprises on a long-term basis, whereas the speculator bought stocks with no other purpose than to play them for a quick rise or fall. The investor who kept his money in businesses that supplied some human need was entitled to a return, but the speculator, whose activities inspired fear and uncertainty, deserved nothing but loss. No one summarized the case against the speculator better than Andrew Carnegie, who approved Wall Street's services to investors but abhorred the speculative side of the Street's activities:

> All pure coins have their counterfeits; the counterfeit of business is speculation. A man in business always gives value in return for his revenue, and thus performs a useful function. His services are necessary and benefit the community; besides, he labours steadily in developing the resources of the country, and thus contributes to the advancements of the race. This is the genuine coin. Speculation, on the contrary, is a parasite fastened upon the labour of business men. It creates nothing and supplies no want. When the speculator wins he takes money without rendering service, or giving value therefor, and when he loses, his fellow-speculator takes the money from him. It is a pure gambling operation between them, degrading to both. You can never be an honest man of business and a speculator.[3]

Carnegie once told a group of business college students that if they wanted to gamble they should "go to a regular and well-conducted house where they cheat fair." [4] Earlier generations of business boys had received similar advice from moralists like Timothy S. Arthur, who insisted that all stock speculations were conducted on principles of chance. "We doubt very much if any man who engages actively in them can be governed by any honest regard for the interests of his fellow man," Arthur declared.[5] Freeman Hunt likewise denounced speculation as a "deep game," and one that led inevitably to fraud. "The history of frauds teaches that they originate chiefly in the attempt to grow rich rapidly by financiering," he observed, "rather than by diligence in business." [6]

One of the main teachings of the success cult was that the only honorable fortunes were those that were built up slowly, on the basis of steady industry. The man who piled up safe, sure gains, had more honor in the cult than the man who tried to get rich quick. "Lasting successes are those which are carefully, even painfully, built up," said John D. Rockefeller, speaking for the entire school of self-help theorists. "Life is not a gamble, and desirable success cannot be won by the turn of a card." [7] If the prudent man of business seemed to move towards wealth less rapidly than the speculator, he consoled himself with the thought that sudden inflations met with sudden collapses.

Despite their awareness that speculators spread ruin far beyond the business community, self-help advisers never suggested that they should be restrained by public authority. Speculators, like other violators of the business ethic, provided for their own automatic punishment under economic law, and the laws of moral retribution. According to this theory no businessman could operate without credit, and no creditor would lend money to a speculator. "The moment a man is known to speculate," said Carnegie, "his credit is impaired, and soon thereafter it is gone." [8] Periodic panics also had their uses, for they separated the speculator from the man who built his fortune on a foundation of honest industry. "Remember that in financial matters, as in everything else, the day of doom cannot be eternally averted," said George C. Lorimer, a Baptist clergyman. "Were it not for the most wholesome return of 'Black Fridays,' seasons of monetary collapse and bankruptcy, the business world would go on, deceiving and being deceived, until it would perish of its own unveracities and impositions." [9] Even if the speculator survived a panic he ultimately encountered some other disaster that deprived him of his ill-gotten gains. The unfailing rule, under God's moral order, was that gamesters died poor.

The same fate awaited the businessman who was dishonest or unfair in his dealings with competitors, customers, or employees. Success advisers always insisted that honesty was the only policy, not just the best. True, dishonest men prospered, but only for a season. In the end they were ruined by creditors, competitors, and other God-appointed agents of justice. Though honesty was a vague concept, not easily applied to specific situations, most success handbooks tried to provide some precepts to guide the businessman in his relations with others.

In his dealings with competitors the moral man of affairs was to be open, fair, and friendly, not deceitful and malevolent. He was not supposed to disregard or deliberately invade the economic rights of others, for he knew that "a *little,* justly gained, is better than *thousands* secured by stealth, or at the expense of another's rights and interests." [10] He took no advantage, even where it was legal to do so, because he understood that advantage-taking, like stealing, involved the appropriation of another's property without his knowledge or consent. Those who raised themselves on the ruin of others advertised that they were ignorant of God's rules for economic life. The correct businessman was the one who applied the Golden Rule to all his dealings with competitors.

The crimes most often perpetrated against customers

consisted of misrepresentation, the sale of shoddy or defective goods, giving short measure, and overcharging. All of these practices were unworthy of men who hoped to make their marks in the world, for as Horace Mann remarked, "The man who sells one thing for another, or less for more, or an inferior for a superior quality, though he may enter a large item on the 'Profit' side of his earthly ledger; yet, in the Book of Life, he will find it entered on the side of 'Loss.' "[11] The dishonest merchant was sure to be found out by the spiritual police and magistrates who maintained moral order in a wicked world. The wise trader, forewarned of the impossibility of evading their awful justice, did not begin the sale of goods to customers by selling his soul to Satan. Customers themselves were agents of moral justice, for they could withold patronage and induce others to do likewise, and thus bring the dishonest merchant to ruin. Because the customer was presumed to have life or death power over a businessman, politeness, like honesty, became a cardinal virtue. This did not mean that the customer was always right, or that the merchant should bow and scrape before him. Politeness was nothing more than an outward expression of charity towards all men. The polite merchant was never obsequious or condescending; he took no account of any man's social position but treated all as Christian brothers. "Do not toady to the rich and browbeat the poor," was his motto. "You cannot judge a man's purse by his coat."[12]

As already noted, the success cult insisted that employees must identify themselves with their masters' interests, advancing those interests in every honorable way. In the reverse application of this doctrine success philosophers laid heavy obligations on employers. "The greatest good of an employer," they warned, "is wrapped up in the highest welfare of his employees. Their interests are identical and cannot be separated. The well-being and contentment of those who make it possible for him to carry on his business form a large part of the assets of an employer; and when he makes plans for their improvement, he is making the most profitable investment he can make for himself." [13] This meant, in the first instance, that the employer was to pay a living wage, enough to take care of every physical necessity and to assure peace of mind. It was not enough simply to pay on the basis of current rates determined by the iron law of wages. Nor did glutted labor markets or the willingness of desperate men to work for less than a subsistence lessen the obligation. When businesses returned large profits, owners were under special obligation to share those profits with their men. A good conscience could be maintained far better by paying decent wages than by donating to big philanthropies. "Millions of the money that is being donated to educational institutions, libraries, hospitals, and other philanthropic purposes, has really been stolen from employees, by clipping it from their wages," Orison Marden declared. "It is true that it was not illegally done, for the employees agreed to work for the amount they received, but this does not cancel the moral obligation of the employer." [14]

Clerks and wage-earners were not to be paid in money alone; they were entitled to recognition and praise for work well done. A responsible master would reward his employees with promotions to positions of greater responsibility, provide them with opportunities for self-improvement, and, when they had proved their worth, help them to become independent businessmen. Even if the hireling lacked ambition and chose to remain with his master through a lifetime, he still deserved kind treatment. The honorable employer, understanding that his men were equals in the sight of God, would treat them as self-respecting human beings, not as animals or machines.

Here again self-help theorists forecast failure for violators of these principles, personal failures which had nothing to do with legal enactments or the activities of trade unions. Low wages, they argued, automatically encouraged dishonesty and faithlessness among employees. "If not cheated of their property," said one critic of low-paying masters, "they are of that honest zeal which a man justly treated delights to exercise in his employer's interests." [15] The prosperity of an employer would be in direct proportion to his generous treatment of employees. The miserly and the unkind could expect to meet financial disaster in this life and spiritual disaster in the next, for exploiters of labor could hope for no mercy at the Throne of Grace. "I would not bear their hearts who have so made money, were the world a solid globe of gold, and mine," said Henry Ward Beecher, "I would not stand for them in the judgment, were every star of Heaven a realm of riches, and mine. I would not walk with them the burning marl of Hell, to bear their torment, and utter their groans, for the throne of God itself." [16]

II

What of social Darwinism in relation to the social precepts of the self-help creed? What of it, indeed! The success cult took its texts from the Bible, not from writings of Darwin and Spencer. It preached no warfare of each against all, but rather a warfare of each man against his baser self. The problem of success was not that of grinding down one's competitors, but of elevating one's self—and the two were not equivalent. Opportunities for success, like opportunities for salvation, were limitless; heaven could receive as many as were worthy. Such a conception of the economic heaven differed from the Malthusian notion that chances were so limited that one man's rise meant the fall of many others. It was this more optimistic view, that every triumph opened the way for more, which dominated the outlook of men who wrote handbooks of self-help.

If there were sufficient opportunities for all, and so it seemed to these optimists, there was no need to explain business relations in terms of the law of the jungle. If the impact of social Darwinism on American thought were judged by the evidence in success handbooks, the judgment would be that it had slight influence. *How to Become Rich,* a tract published anonymously in 1878, stood almost alone in its recommendation to "go in to win" by making use of all available means for scrambling ahead of competitors, but even this recommendation was qualified by the suggestion that the scrambling be done "in a gentlemanly, high-toned way" which would command respect.[17] Andrew Carnegie, a friend of Spencer and a complete Darwinist, talked about the aggressive poor who came into the business world "trained for the contest, with sinews braced, indomitable wills, resolved to do or die." [18] But when he talked about the rules of the contest, and the social justifications of wealth, he stole his lines from the Protestant ethic. In justifying big business combinations John D. Rockefeller once asserted that "The American Beauty rose can be produced . . . only by sacrificing the early buds which grow up around it." [19] But when he was justifying his personal activity he spoke instead of industry, frugality, and sobriety, and of the wealth that came as the reward of virtue. After 1900, when Darwinian ideas had begun to make an impression on the popular mind, an occasional success adviser spoke favorably of getting the jump on competitors, of pushing them down and getting their scalps.[20] Even then, however, wary apologists refused to cast the businessman in the jungle image:

"Business is Business," the Little Man said,
"A battle where 'everything goes'
Where the only gospel is 'get ahead'
And never spare friends nor foes,
'Slay or be slain,' is the slogan cold,
You must struggle and slash and tear,
For Business is Business, a fight for gold,
Where all that you do is fair!

"Business is Business," the Big Man said,
A battle to make of earth
A place to yield us more wine and bread
More pleasure and joy and mirth;
There are still some bandits and buccaneers
Who are jungle-bred beasts of trade,
But their number dwindles with passing years
And dead is the code they made! . . .

"And those who make it a ruthless fight
Have only themselves to blame
If they feel no whit of the keen delight
In playing the Bigger Game,
The game that calls on the heart and head,
The best of man's strength and nerve;
Business is Business," the Big Man said,
"And that Business is to serve!" [21]

The truth of the matter is that social Darwinism did not provide the dominant rationale for American businessmen in the years after the Civil War. America in this period may have appeared as a vast caricature of the Darwinian struggle for existence, as Richard Hofstadter has suggested, but one wonders at the claim that businessmen welcomed "the plausible analogies of social selection, and . . . the expansive evolutionary optimism of the Spencerian system." [22] How many of these men read Darwin or Spencer? How many boasted of their triumphs in terms of ruthless qualities of character? How many advised the young to be strong in tooth and claw? The answer is, precious few. This generation of moneymakers went to school to the Bible, as had earlier generations back as far as the Reformation; it continued the practice of explaining its triumphs in terms of Christian piety. The clichés, mental habits, and intellectual traditions of centuries could not be transformed suddenly by discoveries in the field of biology. Even when Henry Ward Beecher, a popular interpreter of evolution, talked of the problem of business success, he spoke as though Darwin had never been born.

Evolutionary ideas made their way slowly in America, even among the intellectual classes. Darwinism did not gain complete respectability in scientific circles until 1880, and despite the popularizing efforts of John Fiske, Edward Livingston Youmans, and others, it did not very generally dominate the thinking of educated men before about 1900. The authors of self-help propaganda were not learned philosophers, scientists, or social theorists who stood at the forefront of movements of thought, but a very ordinary set of journalists, clergymen, teachers, and businessmen who owed a greater debt to Benjamin

Franklin than to Herbert Spencer. And the audience to whom they addressed themselves were the young and the uninformed, with deep roots in religion and very shallow ones in science. Ambitious boys could understand the man of wealth as a model of virtue and an agent of Christian charity, but they could not understand him in terms of natural selection, and the doctrine of the survival of the fittest. Business practice may have suggested a Darwinian struggle for existence, but the self-help rationale insisted that the only struggle of consequence was the struggle for good character.

III

The success cult's debt to the Protestant ethic is also revealed in its teachings on the purposes and uses of wealth. Like that ethic, it warned that the accumulation of money was justifiable only in terms of the good the money could accomplish for the rest of mankind. "Wealth is nothing only in relation to its uses," said one handbook. "Money is but a representative. . . . It requires some considerable amount of practical philosophy to *make* money, but infinitely more to appropriate it to its only *legitimate uses.*" [23] "We have a right to complain of the rich," said Grover Cleveland, "if, after spending their lives in gathering wealth, they find in its possession no mandate of duty, and no pleasure, save in the inactive and sordid contemplation of their hoard." [24] Private gain became a noble pursuit, losing any taint of avarice, when it advanced the social welfare. Indeed, if the rich man continuously employed his capital in some useful enterprise, society benefited in direct proportion to his earnings.

There was always a danger, however, that the businessman would deceive himself into thinking that society could not survive without his special contributions. Without his realization he could become the servant instead of the master of money, devoting himself to its illusory chase until the day of his death. In the acquisition of wealth, therefore, it was just as important to know when to stop as when to start. "The most miserable of men, as old age approaches, are those who have made money-making their god," Andrew Carnegie declared; "like flies on the wheel, these unfortunates fondly believed they were driving it, only to find when tired and craving rest that it is impossible for them to get off, and they are lost. . . ." [25] In order to avoid this pitfall himself, Carnegie retired from active business while there was still time for him to engage in a different kind of stewardship.

Again, like the Protestant ethic, the success cult endorsed the ancient doctrine of the stewardship of wealth. As God's trustee the rich man was not free to use money as he pleased, he was under obligation to preserve it, enlarge it, and apply it to good works. "I do not recognize myself as owner in fee of one dollar of the wealth which has come into my hands," said Peter Cooper in a characteristic expression of the principle; "I am simply responsible for the management of an estate which belongs to humanity." [26] Most rich Americans of the nineteenth century sooner or later accepted this doctrine. Andrew Carnegie publicized it in 1889 as the "Gospel of Wealth" and as something of a new discovery in the field of social relations. In 1907, after John D. Rockefeller had begun to distribute largesse on a grand scale, he too solemnly affirmed that "Every man owes a debt to humanity, and in accordance with the manner in which he discharges that debt will he be judged." [27] Lesser rich men, hoping to win a favorable judgment on their lives, also tried to establish a record of responsible stewardship through benevolence.

If a man's fortune could only be justified in terms of his service to mankind, then it followed logically that it was not right for him to transmit it to his children. That any man should acquire wealth through the accident of birth was, from a social point of view, indefensible. In addition, success philosophers believed that heirs lacked those qualities of character necessary for a responsible stewardship. The children of the rich were generally pictured as soft, lazy, incompetent, and immoral. Russell Conwell spoke for the entire cult of self-help when he asserted that "It is no help to a young man or woman to inherit money. It is no help to your children to leave them money, but if you leave them education, if you leave them Christian character, if you leave them a wide circle of friends, if you leave them an honorable name, it is far better than that you should leave them money. It would be worse for them, worse for the nation, that they should have any money at all. Oh, young man, if you have inherited money, don't regard it as a help. It will curse you through your years, and deprive you of the very best things of human life. There is no class of people to be pitied so much as the inexperienced sons and daughters of the rich of our generation." [28]

As a brash young man Andrew Carnegie once wrote in a rich lady's album, "I should as soon leave to my son a curse as the almighty dollar." [29] And as an elderly social philosopher he went far beyond other success theorists by advocating inheritance taxes that would make it impossible to transmit fortunes from one generation to the next. "It is difficult to understand why, at the death of its possessor, great wealth . . . should not be shared by the community which has been the most potent cause or partner of all in its creation," Carnegie observed. The steelmaster expressed the hope that some day "under a just system of taxation" such wealth would be restored to the community from whence it came.[30]

Although other success apologists shared Carnegie's conviction, most of them shied away from the remedy of public taxation, holding instead to the popular nineteenth-century theory that the ends of society would best be served if the incompetent sons of the rich were allowed to lose their wealth to the aggressive sons of the poor. "If rich men's sons will not endure the drudgery by which nearly all their fathers secured money and position, they must take a secondary place in the next generation," said a typical handbook; "and oftener they drop out of sight amid the idle, worthless herd, if, indeed they escape an association with loafers and criminals." [31] Theodore Parker claimed that he knew for a fact that, in the years after the Civil War, few of the rich men of Boston were sons of rich men and fewer still were grandsons. As he saw it there was a constant circulation, with the sons of the rich moving towards poverty as the struggling poor moved towards wealth. Matthew H. Smith thought he saw the same process at work in New York: "The sons of princely merchants have become beggars. Men who inherited fortunes from their fathers dwell in tenement houses. A new race of men, who were coal-heavers, porters, errand boys, and clerks of the old merchants, now dwell in palaces, and drive dashing teams through Central Park. Neither in Boston, Philadelphia, or any other of our large cities, has property descended to a third generation, so statistics show." [32] Recent statistics, however, contradict Smith, for they indicate that men who built great fortunes after the

Civil War were extremely successful in transmitting their wealth to later generations. The fortunes of the Vanderbilts, Rockefellers, Mellons, and Fords have shown no diminution through successive generations, and this despite the struggling poor. In addition, in succeeding their fathers as managers of large enterprises these sons of distinguished businessmen have created a more caste-like managerial class, one even less open to invasion from below.[33] Some of these faithless stewards, who thought more of their families than of their fellowmen, appear to have avoided those inevitable disasters and punishments which the self-help creed promised those who sinned by transmitting.

Peter Cooper, Ezra Cornell, and Andrew Carnegie thought that the most sensible stewards were those who gave as much time and thought to the dispensation of wealth as they had to its accumulation. They assumed that men who had earned money the hard way would be as sagacious in giving as in getting, and far more sagacious than executors or administrators who had never won fortunes themselves. This was the basis of Carnegie's famous assertion that the aim of the millionaire should be to die poor, and that those who died rich died disgraced. They were disgraced not only because they had clung to their wealth throughout life, but also because they had left its administration to men less efficient than themselves. To some extent Carnegie fell under his own condemnation, for even though he gave away vast sums, death overtook him before he had divested himself of his entire fortune.

Many authorities argued that God gave riches to a privileged few so they could assist the poor through charity, but hard-headed men like Carnegie sometimes resisted charity on the ground that it encouraged the poor in their vices. "Every drunken vagabond or lazy idler supported by alms bestowed by wealthy people is a source of moral infection to a neighborhood," Carnegie observed. "It will not do to teach the hard-working industrious man that there is an easier path by which his wants can be supplied." [34] Throwing the money into the sea was more preferable to Carnegie than giving it to charity. Though he gave away one hundred twenty-five million dollars between 1887 and 1907, none of it went for the direct relief of the unfortunate classes. As a good Darwinist he saw no reason for trying to save the unfit.

Though other self-made men sometimes gave money for the relief of distress, most of them preferred to use their wealth in ways that opened new opportunities for the ambitious poor. Acting on the premise that "You cannot push any one up a ladder unless he be willing to climb a little himself," [35] donors tried to improve the prospects of those who were already trying to improve themselves. No young man was compelled to use Carnegie's libraries, museums, or music halls; or the universities endowed by Vanderbilt, Cornell, Stanford, and Rockefeller; or the institutes and art galleries organized by Cooper, Peabody, and Mellon. These agencies offered broad opportunities for self-improvement, and through them the self-made men of one generation tried to prepare the way for their successors in the next.

As a social philosopher and spokesman for the well-to-do, Carnegie often claimed that the stewardship of wealth offered the best possible solution to the question of the right relationship of wealth to poverty. Presumably it was the best possible solution because it permitted each man to decide the extent of his obligations for himself.

Those who failed to fulfil their duties would be punished not by man-made laws and courts of justice but by the laws of nature and of nature's God. The businessman had reason to prefer moral regulation to legal regulation, for moral law was remote and somewhat retarded in its operation. If he did not fear a bad conscience, or a bad reputation, or the terrors of hell, he had nothing to fear. But if like Carnegie he cherished a good name, or like Peter Cooper a good conscience, he tried to square his deeds with the social doctrines of the success creed.

More Precious Than Rubies

VI

FROM FRANKLIN'S DAY to our own, self-help advisers have been concerned with the relation of education to business success. This has been a fundamental concern, born of the conviction that the pursuit of fortune is a rational pursuit requiring knowledge and understanding. To the businessman knowledge was more than power, it was wealth itself. The ignorant man could not find his proper calling for he could not analyze his own nature; he did not know how to discipline his character along profitable lines; nor could he recognize Dame Fortune when he saw her or know how to respond to her call. The man who hoped to make his mark in the world had to be able to recognize the ends he was seeking, and above all, the means to those ends. Authors of self-help handbooks attempted to pull aside the curtain of ignorance, and tried, in a general way, to instruct the young in the ways of wealth. They emphasized the advantages of formal schooling, for like other Americans they believed that education could prescribe a cure for many social and personal ills. "Just see," wrote Andrew Carnegie, "wherever we peer into the first tiny springs of the national life, how this true panacea . . . bubbles forth—education, education, education." [1] But did the boy destined for a business career need a special kind of education? Could he find it in the schools? And if he found it, how much of his life should he devote to it?

Until the last decade of the nineteenth century the educational ideal of the business community embraced nothing more than common school training, a business apprenticeship, and a program of self-culture. This was an ideal that squared with the facts of life, for in this era most poor boys could not dream of college training; as late as 1890 the average American had not been educated beyond the fifth grade. In a pre-corporate, pioneering business age sensible men did not expect managers, engineers, accountants, and technicians to come ready-made from the schools. The beginner was qualified if he was able to read, to write a legible hand, and to cipher accurately. Henry Clews got his start in Wall Street when Wilson G. Hunt and Company found his penmanship superior to that of other applicants for the job of assistant bookkeeper. Later, as an employer, Clews made his own preliminary selection of employees by a similar test. Many others started on their way to positions of influence in the nineteenth-century business world with no more than the three R's. Sorokin discovered that of all the American millionaires who rose from humble circumstances, 88.3 percent had no more than a high school education, while 71.7 percent had either only elementary schooling or no formal education at all. Of the eminent businessmen listed in *Who's Who in America* for 1900, 84 percent had not been educated beyond high school.[2] Little wonder that the term "self-made man" assumed an absence of higher learning.

The boy who entered the office from the public school served an apprenticeship of several years, during which he learned numerous routines, mastered the details of the business, and exposed his moral fiber to a toughening process. He literally began at the bottom, sweeping the floors of the office, for most employers believed that if he had the temperament and qualities of the future partner he would not hesitate to try his hand with the broom. In theory, at least, from the broom he would progress to messenger boy, file clerk, shipping clerk, bookkeeper, secretary, and eventually partner. Severe and humbling though this training was, it produced thorough businessmen. Andrew Carnegie boasted such an apprenticeship and took special pleasure in reciting the names of other successful men who had duplicated his experience. With the rise of giant corporations, however, the apprenticeship system died out rapidly, to the dismay of the system's graduates. "There is a great deal to be gained," one graduate said in 1904, "by the discipline of daily life that comes with drudgery, such as the washing of ink-stands, cleaning windows, carrying bundles, and sweeping out the store, although, unfortunately for the boy's own good, the conditions are such at the present that he is not called upon to do that work as was the custom a generation ago." [3]

Young men were usually encouraged to educate themselves through a program of self-culture on the theory that no businessman could learn all he needed to know through experience. If only for the sake of business itself, he was obligated to cultivate the broadest possible knowledge. "You see, gentlemen," Carnegie once told an audience of business hopefuls, "the businessman of this day has to read, yes, and study, and go to the roots of many things, that he may avoid the pitfalls that surround business upon every side." [4] Most authorities agreed that in the early nineteenth century, when the industrial age was just dawning in America, physical prowess had been valued above knowledge among those who performed the world's work. "Fifty years ago men were paid for strength of muscle," a counselor declared in 1878. "That was a gala-day for the giants. Now, muscle is at a discount. . . . Thought is the only thing that can win, and every pursuit is calling for men of mind." [5] James E. Parton, one of the last century's ablest biographers, and an authority on self-made men, also advised the post–Civil-War generation that the reign of stupidity in every field was fast coming to a close; in the new industrial era, he predicted, only those who improved their minds would be able to qualify as managers of great enterprises. Others argued that if the businessman aspired to be known as an agent of progress and a friend of learning, he must increase the breadth of his culture as he increased his fortune. "You must therefore resolve in your mind to enlarge and raise yourself as well," one handbook advised, "you must grow with the growth of your circumstances; you must increase to the stature of the fortune you would possess." [6]

Most of the recommended programs of self-culture had a utilitarian squint. Mathematics, the basic discipline, served as a foundation for such other favored subjects as bookkeeping, surveying, engineering, navigation, chemistry, and natural philosophy. Law, geography, and political economy also had their advocates. Fearing that young men might confine themselves too closely to practical subjects, many writers recommended an exploration of the whole field of human knowledge. The man who sampled all worthy disciplines would improve his intellectual powers, his tastes, and his knowledge. "It matters little what,—a science, an art, a language,—any branch of human knowledge, or industry, or investigation —they are all good." [7] Ordinarily logic was recommended for the sharpening of the intellectual faculties, and moral philosophy for the improving of the moral perceptions. Some advisers also recommended study of modern languages and some acquaintance with history, biography, and books of travel, which would serve at least as an introduction to the great men and events of other lands.

But advice on self-culture, like advice on business ethics, was often ignored by self-made men who were too busy for intellectual pursuits. Despite his urbane manner John Jacob Astor, for example, was scarcely literate; throughout his life he wrote a wretched scrawl, setting spelling and grammar equally at defiance. Daniel Drew, cattle-drover and financier, never took to book-learning and never learned to spell; in school he was always spelled down the first time around. "But I never minded that very much," Drew said. "I never did care two pins what people thought of me." [8] Cornelius Vanderbilt was reputed to have read only one book in his lifetime, Bunyan's *Pilgrim's Progress,* and he read it after he was seventy years of age.

By contrast, Andrew Carnegie represented the self-culture ideal at its best. As a working boy he borrowed books regularly from the private library of Colonel James Anderson of Allegheny, and as a mature businessman he read widely in history, politics, economics, and philosophy. Carnegie brought Matthew Arnold to America, cultivated John Morley and Lord Bryce, and maintained the closest of relations with Herbert Spencer. Ezra Cornell associated with Louis Agassiz, James Russell Lowell, and Goldwyn Smith on terms of equality, and played an

active role with Andrew Dixon White in planning and founding Cornell University. George Peabody maintained a lifelong interest in affairs of the mind, and possessed a breadth of culture that enabled him to move easily in the best London society. Nathaniel Hawthorne, who knew both English and American self-made men, may have had Peabody in mind when he argued that the English self-made man remained uncouth throughout life, whereas the American was "not distinguishable outwardly, and perhaps as refined within, as nine tenths of the gentlemen born, in the House of Commons." [9]

Self-made men sometimes identified themselves with the ideal of self-culture by using their money to endow institutions that encouraged self-improvement. After 1820 businessmen of the principal Eastern cities subsidized mercantile libraries, where clerks and mechanics could gather in the evenings for reading and lectures. In leading business centers, like New York, these libraries were well attended.[10] One of the few benefactions of tight-fisted John Jacob Astor was the Astor Library, which opened in New York in 1854. In the last half of the century, when the public library movement reached its peak, Ezra Cornell, Andrew Carnegie, and other self-made men gave it liberal support, in the belief that libraries served as ladders for the upward climb of the aspiring poor. Peter Cooper went even further when he organized the Cooper Union in New York, where young men of the working classes could study mathematics, mechanics, chemistry, electricity, and drawing. Thanks to the Union's program of free lectures, they had access to the greatest men and greatest minds of the age. Shortly before his death in 1869 George Peabody provided similar benefits for the working classes of Baltimore. In addition to a library, the Peabody Institute maintained a program of lectures, an academy of music, and an art gallery.

Nineteenth-century self-help theorists were only making a virtue of a necessity when they insisted that a businessman could learn all he needed to know by attending a common school, serving an apprenticeship, and pursuing a program of self-culture. Since few poor boys could hope for more, it would have been absurd to prescribe higher qualifications. Besides, did not the richest men of the age offer living proof that a rudimentary education was sufficient unto success?

II

Until the 1890s business opinion ran heavily against higher learning, and men who posed as experts in these matters took special pleasure in pointing out the slight representation of college graduates in the ranks of the elite. When Moses Y. Beach published his list of the wealthiest men of New York in 1842 he called attention to the fact that there were few educated men among them. Fifty years later, another publicist, Edward Bok, asserted that virtually all the great city's business leaders were graduates of the college of hard knocks. Edwin T. Freedley went still further, declaring in 1881 that he doubted that more than six college graduates could be found among the prominent businessmen of the United States. Andrew Carnegie delighted in similar statistics. After jotting down the names of America's leading financiers, merchants, and manufacturers, he concluded that in every department of affairs it was the non-college man who took highest honors. Under onetime clerks and mechanics Carnegie found college men working as salaried subordinates. Allowances must be made for exaggeration in these personal estimates, of course, but later and more reliable evidence confirmed them in general.[11]

Men who claimed that college training was not necessary for success went even further by contending that it was positively harmful in that it unfitted men for business. In an address at the Cooper Union in 1867 Horace Greeley told an audience of business hopefuls that although there were only a few unemployed laboring men in New York City there were at least a thousand jobless college graduates, some with degrees from German universities, men who were not only unemployed but also unemployable because their training had made them unfit for even the humblest positions. Edwin T. Freedley believed that colleges had "directly and indirectly ruined a greater number of their sons than they had ever benefitted," and Andrew Carnegie, reflecting on the relation of education to business, contended that "college education as it exists seems almost fatal to success in that domain." [12] Edward Bok also condemned the colleges on the ground that none of them had ever made a businessman, while all of them had ruined thousands for practical careers.

What was the basis for such attacks? One element of it was the belief that higher learning undermined the rugged personal qualities necessary for success. Success demanded a strong will, diligence, persistence, ambition, good health, and self-discipline, qualities which colleges allegedly crippled and dwarfed in their concentration on the development of mental faculties. Some observers argued that few young men left college with their health unimpaired, while others expressed concern over the morals of those who spent four years in the fleshpots of college. There was a widespread feeling that no college man could qualify as a paragon of moral virtue, so, consequently no prospective creditor or employer would trust him. He was also thought to be deficient in determination, drive, and backbone. "It is not book-learning young men need, nor instruction about this and that," proclaimed Elbert Hubbard, "but stiffening of the vertebrae which will cause them to be loyal to a trust, to act promptly, concentrate their energies: do the thing—'Carry a message to Garcia.' "[13] The college man, like the genius, was thought to be awkward, hypersensitive, impatient, conceited, pedantic, confused, tactless, bookish, and utterly impractical. Daniel Drew never allowed his educated employees to indulge in "bookish airs," because he knew that he could buy them out ten times over. "Book learning is something," said Drew, "but thirteen million dollars is also something, and a mighty sight more."[14] Even Charles F. Thwing, a university president who was in favor of college training for businessmen, conceded that colleges could do less to mold dominating personalities than dominating minds.

Critics of college training denounced the classical curriculum with special vehemence, emphasizing its impracticality and remoteness from everyday life. It was a common feeling that the vast majority of American colleges remained silent on the point of practicality "as though to do battle with life's stern realities were a secondary interest, and, as though to mention the subject in the hours sacred to mathematics, Greek, and Hebrew, were sinful and degrading."[15] Andrew Carnegie openly denounced the kind of education that emphasized the "dead languages," and the history of "petty and insignificant skirmishes between savages." Classical learning might fit men for life upon some other planet, he argued, but it had nothing to do with life on earth.[16] Even James A. Garfield, who had, himself, been exposed to the classics, objected to any curriculum which encouraged American youth to "feed their spirits on the life of dead ages, instead of the inspiring life and vigor of our own times." [17] Thomas Mellon opposed classical learning on the ground that it was difficult to acquire and easy to lose. And there were others, who shared the same opposition but arrived at their conclusion by a different reasoning. Edwin T. Freedley, for example, believed that impractical knowledge burdened a man's mind throughout life, and robbed it of its natural vigor and elasticity. Presumably, too, the classical studies inspired a speculative and theoretical turn of mind that had no place in business.[18]

One of the weightiest objections was that college training devoured the most valuable years of a young man's life. Between the ages of sixteen and twenty, while practical boys were learning in the school of experience, college men were wasting their time on the classics. If the graduate entered business immediately after taking his degree he had to begin at the bottom, broom in hand, four years later than the boy who had gone directly from the public school to the office. The college man, therefore, suffered a hopeless disadvantage, for "The prize takers have too many years the start of the graduate; they have entered for the race invariably in their teens—in the most valuable of all the years for learning—from fourteen to twenty; while the college student has been learning a little about the barbarous and petty squabbles of the past . . . the future captain of industry is hotly engaged in the school of experience, obtaining the very knowledge required for his future triumphs." [19] When a friend of Cornelius Vanderbilt told him that Lord Palmerston, the British statesman, had said it was a pity that a man of his ability had not had the advantage of formal schooling, Vanderbilt snapped back "You tell Lord Palmerston from me that if I had learned education I would not have had time to learn anything else." [20]

Many felt that college boys started their careers with the erroneous idea that their diplomas were passports to quick success. Experience had taught Frederick Weyerhaeuser, the lumber king, that the holder of a degree was "apt to think that because he is a college graduate he ought not be obliged to begin at the bottom of the ladder and work up, as the office boy does who enters the office when he is fourteen years of age." [21] Few college men seemed enthusiastic about washing inkstands, running errands, and sweeping offices, and few seemed happy to learn the lessons taught in the college of hard knocks. President John W. Dunn of the International Steam Pump Company issued a standard warning when he declared that "Any young man . . . who is imbued with a belief that because he has gone through college he has nothing further to learn . . . will find that his college education is not only of no benefit to him, but is a positive hindrance to his success in life." [22]

Despite such complaints, it would be a mistake to assume that there were no limits to the nineteenth-century businessman's hostility to the higher learning. Titans who denounced college training as a fit preparation for business sometimes spoke generously of its value as a preparation for professional or other non-business careers. A few even confessed that their lack of education gave them some feelings of social inadequacy. "Folks may say that I don't care about education; but it ain't true; I do," hard-bitten Commodore Vanderbilt confided to a clergyman.

"I've been to England, and seen them lords, and other fellows, and knew that I had twice as much brains as they had maybe, and yet I had to keep still, and couldn't say anything through fear of exposing myself." [23] Frederick Weyerhaeuser, who criticized higher learning on many counts, admitted, however, that it must be a source of lifelong satisfaction to its possessor. Andrew Carnegie, who as a prosperous young man had toyed with the idea of attending Oxford, recommended college training for all who could afford it simply for its social and intellectual advantages. "Liberal education," Carnegie said, "gives a man who really absorbs it higher tastes and aims than the acquisition of wealth, and a world to enjoy, into which the mere millionaire cannot enter; to find therefore that it is not the best training for business is to prove its claim to a higher domain." [24]

The businessman's passion for educating his children, and for endowing colleges, indicated some contradiction of his opposition to higher learning. President Charles W. Eliot of Harvard observed that when a man's success enabled him to underwrite a liberal education for his children, he provided such an education, regardless of future careers,[25] for the prestige of a college education overrode any limitations of business training. Rockefeller, Carnegie, Vanderbilt, Drew, Cornell, and Stanford were not averse to supporting such institutions; they gladly transformed their wealth into seats of learning, believing their lives to be dignified thereby. Long before the educational values of the business community were revolutionized practical men in search of prestige willingly gave their substance to promote that which they purported to despise.

III

As the nineteenth century gave way to the twentieth the educational prejudices of the older generation of business leaders gradually diminished. No overnight revolutions occurred, of course, for in the realm of ideas change comes slowly and in piecemeal fashion. But sensitive observers agreed that there was less bias against college men in 1900 than there had been a decade earlier, just as there was to be less in each decade thereafter. In the fall of 1903 when the Mosely Educational Commission came from Great Britain to study the relationship of education to prosperity in the United States, businessmen told the investigators that whereas few employers had been willing to hire college graduates in 1890, many had developed a preference for them by 1900. The Pennsylvania Railroad, for example, had just adopted regulations requiring all new appointees to executive positions to have college training in engineering, and all officers aspiring to future promotion to possess some kind of college degree.[26]

The central fact behind this tendency was the coming of age of the American economic system. The pioneer mercantile, industrial, and financial operations of the post–Civil-War years had been handled by practical, strong-willed men who were more distinguished for ruggedness of character than for refinement of intellect. In an age of abundant opportunities, daring, coupled with rule-of-thumb methods, had often proved sufficient unto success. At the century's close, however, businessmen were less concerned with pioneering than with the expansion and maintenance of their complex empires. It was not easy to sustain and operate giant corporations on the basis of hunch and mistake. The college of hard knocks was no longer equal to the task of training men for leadership in a corporate age. Frederick D. Underwood, who rose from the ranks to become president of the Erie Railroad, put the matter bluntly when he announced in 1903 that "The demand for technical skill and commercial ability has lessened the promotion of men from the ranks, and must . . . continue to do so." [27] Even to men outside the business community the new tendency was apparent. In 1897, when Grover Cleveland addressed the students of Princeton University on the role of the self-made man in American life, he pointed to the rapid decline of the old superstition concerning the close relationship of the self-made man and meager educational advantages, and indicated that in all lines of activity the future belonged to the college man. A year later a Milwaukee clergyman told a group of business boys, "You might as well expect to learn the business of *medicine* simply from the practice, without preliminary study, as to learn business, as carried on today, by *experience,* without any training in technical business education." [28]

As corporations replaced the personal dynasties built up by self-made men, college graduates had less and less difficulty in getting themselves accepted. Corporations were reluctant to wait for office boys to "come through"; they preferred to manufacture their officers quickly, using universities, law schools, and technical schools to this end. The formation of the United States Steel Corporation in 1901 was symbolic in this connection, for it brought about the retirement of Andrew Carnegie, a long-time critic of the college man, and elevated Judge Elbert H. Gary, a lawyer and graduate who shared none of Carnegie's educational prejudices. According to James B. Dill, the famed corporation lawyer, virtually all the leading combines rearranged their men at the turn of the century on the theory that those with college training were most valuable. As Dill saw it, the corporate tendency had set at rest the discussion as to whether college training was essential to business success. "It has answered the question in the affirmative," Dill said, "because the demand today for trained minds, devoted to specific lines of work, has created a demand for college trained men." [29] The demand was still new at the time Dill wrote, for the rapid development of corporations came after 1896, but it was an insistent demand that spelled a better future for degree holders. William Miller's recent study of the men who managed the largest corporations in the first decade of this century showed that 29 percent had college degrees, and another 12 percent had some college training. This was but a foretaste of the future. By 1923 almost 32 percent of all businessmen listed in *Who's Who in America* held college degrees, and 45 percent had some college experience. At mid-century there were reports that nearly 80 percent of the nation's top business leaders had come from the campus.[30] Whatever the elements of exaggeration in these statistics, the trend was unmistakable.

Another factor contributing to the new enthusiasm for higher learning after 1900 was the widespread recognition that opportunities were less plentiful than in the years immediately after the Civil War. Soothsayers could not conceal the fact that the frontier had closed, that the nation's basic resources had long since been appropriated, and that small enterprisers had been put on the defensive by big business. The movement towards consolidation meant that in the new era there would be fewer heads of concerns, and more men relegated to positions of secondary influence. There was still room at the top, but in the years after 1900 men were increasingly concerned about the number of places at the bottom. As competition for top positions became more severe, employers raised standards of qualification by requiring degrees of those who hoped to rise into the managerial ranks. Industrial leaders advised the Mosely Educational Commission in 1903 that even though the uneducated youth of outstanding ability might still win an occasional executive position, his chances were rapidly diminishing. The same estimate was heard on every side:

> The unlearned and uneducated man will always have his place in this world of ours; but yet he will not hereafter have such opportunities . . . the man who would succeed, in whatever rank of business life, in whatever profession, must hereafter meet in competition men who, in addition to all the energy, vigor and ambition which he may display, will have a brain stored with knowledge and scientifically cultivated and trained, and thus far better equipped than formerly for successful struggles with the world and for seizing opportunities and meeting the responsibilities of the highest positions for which all may strive.[31]

Orison Marden, sensing the drift, advised young men to "restrain" the desire to go to work until they had piled up considerable success capital in the form of education. And Powell Stackhouse, an officer of the Cambria Steel Company, told all young men entering the steel industry to get an education, "as without it a limit of advancement will sooner or later be reached." [32]

Such advice would have been meaningless, of course,

if aspirants had not been able to find in the schools the kind of training that practical men could respect. Thanks to the educational revolutions of the last thirty years of the nineteeenth century, business boys could learn in the school what they had previously learned on the job. With the rise of commercial colleges young men could get training in routines without serving an extended office apprenticeship. The rapid growth of such schools indicated that they met a genuine need. As late as 1870 there were only twenty-six commercial colleges in the entire United States, but by 1894 there were more than five hundred, serving almost a hundred thousand students. Self-help advisers welcomed the appearance of such schools, and spoke favorably of their services. James A. Garfield, for example, told a group of commercial graduates in 1869 that they had received better training for the practical business of life than the graduates of Harvard, Yale, and Princeton.[33] Employers were less enthusiastic at first, for they could not conceive that business routines could be taught off the job. But by the turn of the century this misapprehension had disappeared, and graduates of the "clerk factories" found a ready market for their skills.

Meantime technical schools had begun to supply more highly trained masters of machinery. Their superior performance on the job helped weaken the old prejudice against all forms of higher education. In 1860 there were only six schools of technology in the United States, but by 1900 there were forty-two. At first industrialists had their doubts about graduates of these institutions, but in face of the tangible evidence of their worth, skepticism gave way to appreciation. "It took 15 years to persuade manufacturers of the value of our men," one technical school official testified. "It was a long hard struggle. But they know it now." [34] As indeed they did for after the turn of the century many industrialists commented appreciatively on the work of the universities in technical fields. George A. Warburton, a railroad official, predicted in 1903 that thereafter railroads would recruit most of their leading men from the technical schools. John D. Rockefeller contended that industrial concerns in every field would follow the same practice, for he believed that the technical school had made "the upward course of the earnest, willing-to-work young man straight and clear." [35] Andrew Carnegie, who had long proclaimed the superiority of the apprenticed mechanic, had changed his mind as early as 1890: "The trained mechanic of the past, who has . . . hitherto carried on most of the honours in our industrial works, is now to meet a rival in the scientifically educated youth, who will push him hard—very hard indeed." As Carnegie saw it, technical school graduates were more open-minded in respect to new ideas, methods, and machinery than were the old mechanics. "The scientific attitude of mind, that of the searcher after truth, renders them receptive of new ideas," he said. Like other industrialists, Carnegie appreciated this new kind of higher learning because it represented a radical departure from the old classical program. "We have begun to realize that a knowledge of chemistry . . . is worth a knowledge of all the dead languages that ever were spoken upon the earth," he observed, "a knowledge of mechanics more useful than all the classical learning that can be crammed into young men at college." [36] To extend this more useful education he endowed the Carnegie Institute of Technology at Pittsburgh in 1900.

Collegiate schools of business provided still another form of training for the prospective man of affairs. Whereas business colleges concentrated on training men for routine office work, the collegiate school of business tried to prepare its graduates for executive positions. The Wharton School of Finance and Economy blazed the way at the University of Pennsylvania in 1881, and other institutions, such as California, Chicago, and Wisconsin, followed suit after 1898. By the time the Harvard Graduate School of Business Administration was organized in 1908, business education had attained a complete professional status. The business community, adjusting its expectations to the new educational opportunities, made no secret of its preference for college men. "The day has quite gone by," said the *Commercial and Financial Chronicle* in 1916, "when it is sufficient for a young man to begin at the bottom and, without more training than he can gather in the daily routine, to grow up to be something more than a manager of an existing concern, or to acquire that breadth of knowledge and completeness of training which are necessary if he is to be fitted to compete with the expert young business men produced in other countries." [37]

It would be a mistake to assume that business leaders approved only technical and commercial training, for in many quarters after the turn of the century even liberal education found favor. Elbert H. Gary contended that the aspiring businessman could find profit in any kind of general education. "In fact," said Gary, "the more he knows of that which is taught in schools, colleges and universities of a general character, the better it will be for him in commencing business." [38] And there were other executives who gradually came around to the view that industrial leaders needed to be trained as liberally as if they were preparing for one of the learned professions. An observer from the University of Berlin, aware of this new interest in liberal learning, concluded that what American businessmen wanted from the colleges was not more technical assistance, but the kind of training that would enable them to participate in intellectual activities previously monopolized by the aristocratic classes. Men of affairs seemed anxious to "secure their share of the ideal possessions of the nation." [39] Whatever the merits of this observation, business leaders certainly hoped that college graduates would come to them equipped with something more than a knowledge of commercial and industrial routines. They were looking for originality, breadth of vision, and theoretical capacities not often found, and less often honored, among uneducated self-made men.

Despite these impressive concessions to higher learning, anti-college sentiments were not completely swept away. Foreign observers, sensitive to the changing climate of opinion in American business circles, also noticed the persistence of traditional ideas. "That the movement in favor of higher education in America is pushing vigorously ahead is quite undeniable," one such investigator reported in 1905. "Nevertheless, in that land of 'self-made men' the opposition can not be said to have died out." [40] Charles M. Schwab, a college man himself, was a case in point. In 1917 Schwab repeated all the old shibboleths about the defects of college men, with special emphasis on the complaint that they wasted their evenings with music, society, and the theater, when they should have been improving their time with work and study. But even Schwab had to admit that time had already run out on his kind of man. "Whatever may have been true in the past," he conceded, "there is no doubt that to-day industrial conditions favor the college man." [41] Which was another way of saying that industrial conditions no longer favored the self-made man.

Preach the Gospel

VII HAD THERE BEEN no printing presses, forums, or pulpits in nineteenth-century America, popular worship of material success might have been less intense, but it would have been no less real. Success worship did not depend primarily upon propaganda, but upon opportunity; even the most insensitive men must have been aware that there were opportunities aplenty in the new industrial age. Though Thomas Mellon went to the city to seek his fortune after reading the life of Benjamin Franklin, many thousands made the same move without ever taking a book in hand. Wherever the industrial revolution transformed the physical basis of life, success was in the air and on men's tongues. "Two men can hardly meet," said Governor Charles Henry Bell of New Hampshire in 1881, "without comparing views respecting some one who has risen to be a public character by originating a new invention, by planning a shrewd speculation, by gaining a fortune, or by distancing competition in the political race." [1] Success sermons and guidebooks reflected a widespread interest in the game of getting on, but they were not the causes of that interest. Self-help homilies fanned the passion for wealth, but they did not give it birth.

The dependence of the success cult on forces within the economy can be read in the record of its publications.

Of all the success manuals published before the year 1900, four out of five appeared after the Civil War, at the very time the American industrial revolution was approaching its climax. "Handbooks and manuals pointing out the highroad to prosperity flourished as never before," said Louis B. Wright, commenting on this literary phenomenon. "Book agents invaded every village and hamlet, even on the most distant frontier, with prospectuses of books guaranteed to supply axioms conducive to prosperity. If any youth of the Gilded Age failed to achieve a position of wealth and eminence, it was not for lack of printed advice. . . ." [2] Even more striking was the fact that at least four out of every five of these manuals originated in the industrial North and East, usually in the great urban centers where fortunes were made. True, publishing facilities were superior in cities like New York and Boston, but this fact can scarcely serve as the whole explanation. Many success manuals were printed privately or in obscure shops; since they were not dependent upon any city's special facilities, they could have been published elsewhere as easily. But the deities and high priests of the cult were men of the industrial states. Who were the southern or western millionaires who could stand beside John Jacob Astor, Peter Cooper, A. T. Stewart, or John D. Rockefeller? In the matter of pointing out the way to wealth, who were the rural publicists who could match pens with Freeman Hunt, Horatio Alger, Elbert Hubbard, and Orison Marden? Americans of the last century may have thought of opportunity in terms of the West and the frontier, but success tracts did not reflect any such faith.[3]

The presence of wealthy self-made men in the North and East probably accounted for the lead these sections assumed in the field of success publicity. Of course most of these men were too busy, too disinterested, or too illiterate to take up the pen in defense of self-help, but a few found it to their taste. *The Life of P. T. Barnum, Written by Himself* (1854) was a best seller in its day, partly owing to the great showman's practice of selling it to the crowds that visited his museum and circus; it went through many editions, passed under various titles, and may have sold as many as half a million copies altogether.[4] Barnum scored lesser triumphs with *The Art of Money-Getting* (1882), *How I Made Millions* (1884), and *Dollars and Sense* (1890), each of which purported to give the novice helpful hints on success. The founder of the Mellon banking fortune imitated the autobiographical style of his hero, Benjamin Franklin, in *Thomas Mellon and His Times* (1885), but his story never reached a large audience. Henry Clews enjoyed greater favor with his memoirs, *Twenty Eight Years in Wall Street* (1887), a veritable mine of information about the Street's successful operators. John D. Rockefeller's *Random Reminiscences of Men and Events* (1909) was more pious, and thoroughly orthodox in its wealth-through-virtue theme. Andrew Carnegie gave the world a vigorous and thoughtful defense of self-help values in *The Gospel of Wealth* (1900) and *The Empire of Business* (1902), as well as in his *Autobiography* (1920). When wealthy men wrote about success they served the cult well, for who was better informed on moneymaking than men who had made it? Their advice was just as improbable as that offered by clergymen and journalists, but it appeared to be more authentic.

By putting themselves in the hands of professional

publicists even the least articulate of these businessmen helped to promote self-help ideas. John Jacob Astor could not write of his own triumphs, but he commanded the pen of Washington Irving. "He began his career, of course, on the narrowest scale," said Irving in his eulogy of the fur trader, "but he brought to the task a persevering industry, rigid economy, and strict integrity. To these were added an aspiring spirit that always looked upwards; a genius bold, fertile, and expansive; a sagacity quick to grasp and convert circumstances to its advantage, and a singular and never wavering confidence of a signal success." [5] Freeman Hunt, Edward Bok, Orison Marden and other prominent journalists used the same resounding clichés when they analyzed the careers of moneymakers for the popular press. In the Gilded Age it was a poor newspaper or magazine that did not publish portraits of the rich, sketches of their lives, estimates of their fortunes, and pictures of their dwellings. As a contemporary remarked, "Kings have no private life, it is said; but no king can live more consistently in the public eye than some of these successful Americans." [6] A few titans, like J. P. Morgan and John D. Rockefeller, refused to be interviewed on the subject of success, but even Rockefeller broke down eventually. In the summer of 1906, while vacationing in France, he unburdened himself to a journalistic "companion of his leisure hours" who jotted down his success homilies and presented them to the public through the pages of the *Cosmopolitan*.

In their quest for new material authors of self-help manuals frequently interviewed the wealthy and bombarded them with questionnaires. Many of their questions were routine, but many more were prejudicial. Was your boyhood spent in the country, or in a city? Did you work as a boy? Did you use tobacco previous to the age of sixteen? Are you a church member? Is honesty necessary to business success? Should a boy be forced into college against his will? Should a country boy go to the big city if chances of success are fair in his own community? To what do you attribute your success? What maxims or watchwords have had a strong influence on your life and helped you to success? What books would you recommend to an ambitious boy? Around the answers to such questions some of the most popular self-help guides were built.[7]

Like the clergy who glorified self-made men, journalists who wrote on success had easy access to the business community. As already noted, Freeman Hunt spoke for the merchants of New York, and Edwin T. Freedley represented the manufacturing interests of Philadelphia. William Mathews, who wrote *Getting On in the World* (1874), was a Chicago financial editor. Edward Bok, author of *Successward* (1899), traveled successward himself by marrying Mary Louise Curtis, daughter of Cyrus Curtis, the wealthy publisher. Orison Marden, whose *Pushing to the Front* (1894) went through two hundred and fifty editions, had made and lost a small fortune in the hotel business before he began telling others how to get rich. Despite their business connections, not many of these journalists achieved wealth, and fewer still had the grace to be embarrassed about giving advice on an art they had not mastered. William Mathews brushed his embarrassment aside with the assertion that a sign can point the way to the traveler "though it has never hopped off upon its one leg and traveled the road to which it points. . . ."[8] Another self-help adviser, T. D. MacGregor, claimed that his publishers told him not to worry about his financial status so long as his advice was orthodox, because, said the publishers, "That's just the kind of stuff that Rockefeller and Carnegie are always getting off." [9] Only the cynical admitted that they wrote success manuals in the hope of making money. The cynic who wrote *About Money* (1872) admitted that "my principal reason for publishing is to relieve my pocket of a general debility," but he hid his name and his shame behind the improbable pseudonym of Ham Jones. Henry Livingston frankly called his book *The Money-Maker* (1868), and told his readers that "The book has been gotten up with the sole object of making money easily and honorably—as well for the Publisher as for the Purchaser. . . ." [10] Such honesty was rare, for most writers pretended to have some noble purpose in mind.

II

In an age of oratory, success lectures were at least as popular as written manuals and constituted one of the most important means of propagating self-help ideas. Here again the North and East had an advantage, for most of the lyceums, mercantile library associations, business colleges, and other sponsoring agencies were concentrated in this section. In the urban centers mercantile library associations, in addition to providing inspirational reading matter, sponsored such lectures by eminent persons. During the 1840s Horace Mann and Edward Everett lectured to the Boston association on self-help, while another Yankee, William Ellery Channing, traveled all the way to Philadelphia to talk success to the members of the Philadelphia Mercantile Library Company. Business colleges were especially active. Matthew H. Smith addressed Comer's Commercial Institute of Boston on *The Elements of Business Success* in June, 1854, then turned over his text to Freeman Hunt for dissemination to a wider audience through the July issue of *Hunt's Merchants' Magazine*. Horace Greeley's *Success in Business,* delivered privately to the students of Packard's Bryant-Stratton New York Business College in November, 1867, attracted so much attention that the lecture hall was crowded almost to suffocation and scores had to be turned away. To satisfy the disappointed, Greeley gave a repeat performance in Cooper Union Hall, which seated twenty-five hundred persons. When again many listeners had to be turned away, the head of the college, S. S. Packard, asked Greeley's permission to publish the address. Greeley gave his assent on the ground that "There are millions of young men in our country who need to know what I tried to say." [11] James A. Garfield's *Elements of Success,* delivered to the Spencerian Business College of Washington, D. C. at its June exercises in 1869, likewise found favor when printed in pamphlet form. Pittsburgh's Curry Commercial College provided expert advice for its graduates in 1885 by inducing Andrew Carnegie to speak on *The Road to Business Success.* The frugal Scot saved the talk for seventeen years, then used it as the opening essay in *The Empire of Business.*

If mercantile libraries and commercial colleges had stood alone in sponsoring such orations the success cult's appeal would have seemed narrow indeed. But there were many sponsoring agencies outside the business community. In the summer of 1848 the Alumni Association of Columbian College, a liberal arts school in Washington, D. C., heard Robert C. Cushman on the enduring theme, *Elements of Success.* On the occasion of Princeton University's 151st anniversary in 1897, Grover Cleveland talked not of the glories of Princeton, but rather of *The Self-Made Man in American Life.* At the University of Pennsylvania the unveiling of a statue to Benjamin Franklin in 1914 provided the occasion for an inspirational address on *The Youthful Franklin,* by James M. Beck, a prominent corporation counsel. Beck was an old hand at this sort of thing, for in 1897 he talked on *Stephen Girard, Merchant and Mariner* at the time of the unveiling of a statue to Philadelphia's first great merchant prince. Men who traveled the popular lecture circuits usually had at least one self-help oration in their repertoires. Edward Bok scored a hit with his *Keys to Success* during the seasons of 1898–1900, and Russell Conwell made a tidy fortune off his all-time classic *Acres of Diamonds* which he delivered more than six thousand times. Churches also sponsored the success gospel as part of their regular service. On February 7, 1892, the Church of the Divine Paternity in New York invited Andrew Carnegie to its pulpit so this well-known sinner and doubter could preach his *Gospel of Wealth.* In 1898 Charles P. Masden of Milwaukee turned the tables on the commercial colleges by inviting the faculty and students of the Spencerian Business College to his church to hear a sermon on *The Sacredness of Business.*

Perhaps the most influential of all forums were the classrooms of the public schools, where teachers had endless opportunities to instruct the young in the ways of success. When the cult of self-help was at its peak there was general agreement, inside and outside the educational community, that schools should be used to this end. It was a poor success philosopher who did not urge teachers to pay special attention to their responsibilities in this field. "It should be persistently impressed upon the mind of a child that the sole object (so far as we can see) of the gift of life to him is that he may make a success of it," said one adviser.[12] Orison Marden offered exactly the same counsel. "If you are a teacher," he advised, "try to impress success-thoughts upon your pupil. Teach him that he is a success-acorn, and that the Creator intended him to unfold into an oak—not a gnarled or dwarfed oak, but a magnificent giant of the forest that will furnish shade for men and beast and timber for a ship or house. Impress upon the child your faith in him; tell him that you expect great things of him in the future, and charge him not to disappoint you." [13] Such exhortations pleased businessmen who believed that they should not bear the entire burden of informing the young of the opportunities around them, and besides educators were perfectly willing to assume the responsibility. "Good teachers aim to establish self-help," said William Makepeace Thayer, one of the giants of the educational movement. "Their ingenuity and patience are often taxed heavily to remove indifference, laziness, slang, deceit, vulgarity, irreverence, and other barriers to success." [14]

Since the public education movement was the by-product of many of the same social forces that produced the self-made man, it was natural that its leaders, such as Horace Mann and Henry Barnard, should have identified themselves with the self-help tradition. Horace Mann was a self-made man himself, and a friend of all the moral virtues that helped the lowly to make their way in the world. He believed that the schools should awaken the young to the "duty of accumulation," but like other moralists of the golden mean he warned against excessive devotion to this duty. His rule was that "all above a fortune is a misfortune." [15] Henry Barnard went far beyond Mann in accepting the business definition of success, and in attempting to use the schools to develop those personal qualities and attitudes that were cherished by employers in the industrial world. Another Yankee educator, William A. Alcott, was even more active in the field of success publicity, through his *Young Man's Guide* (1833), which passed through sixteen editions in eleven years, and *Tall Oaks from Little Acorns* (1856), one of the more thoughtful book-length treatments of the self-help theme. Samuel G. Goodrich, who sold millions of school textbooks in his day, was far better known than Alcott, not only because of his Peter Parley stories, but also because of his *Lives of Benefactors* (1845) and numerous other success handbooks. In the last half of the nineteenth century William Makepeace Thayer achieved the same kind of popularity by writing widely used texts, and grinding out biographies of self-made politicians and businessmen. In 1893–1894 he capped his efforts with a high school text on the *Ethics of Success* and a middle grades version featuring "inspiring anecdotes" from the lives of self-made men. Some of these anecdotes were drawn from the life of Benjamin Franklin, always a favorite in the classroom. We shall never know how many students read Franklin's *Autobiography,* or his maxims, but their number must have been legion. In 1906, when the city of Boston commemorated the anniversary of Franklin's birth by publishing extracts from his writings for use in the public schools, the city fathers were simply living up to a great educational tradition.[16]

Whatever Franklin's influence, it was no more pervasive than that of William Holmes McGuffey, the Ohio schoolmaster whose texts outranked all others in popularity from 1836 until the end of the century. Perhaps as many as half the children in America went to school to McGuffey in this period, and learned industry, frugality, and sobriety from him. The McGuffey readers contained the same synthesis of Christian and middle-class virtues that could be found in the leading manuals on success. This synthesis, present in the first readers, persisted through all editions and revisions, so that through the end of the nineteenth century boys who had access to McGuffey had no need of Horatio Alger or Edward Bok.[17] And boys who had access to none of these giants had nothing to fear, for in the Gilded Age success and her prophets were everywhere.

III

What were the peculiar qualities and forms that characterized the voluminous literature that called young men to the quest for wealth? Most advisers presented their message of triumph in a small package—an essay, address, sermon, or chapter in a book. The essentials, having to do with industry, frugality, and sobriety, could be set forth in a few words. Authors might pad their recommendations with anecdotes, maxims, and instances, but for the most part what they had to say could be said simply and briefly. "Upon a subject which so many pens have discussed, it is, of course, hardly possible to say anything absolutely new," one author admitted; "the most that a writer can hope to do is to recombine and present in novel and attractive forms . . . thoughts that have been substantially repeated from the days of Solomon. . . ."[18] Benjamin Franklin had demonstrated the possibilities of the brief, pungent essay when he published "The Way to Wealth" in *Poor Richard's Almanack* in 1736. In the nineteenth century some of the shortest pieces were the best, such as Elbert Hubbard's *A Message to Garcia* and Russell Conwell's *Acres of Diamonds.* Prior to 1850 few writers devoted entire books to the self-help theme; usually a chapter in a moral handbook was enough for the elaboration of the argument. In *The Young Man's Guide* (1833), for example, William A. Alcott devoted one chapter to "The Management of Business" and six others to the formation of character, amusements and indulgences, improvement of the mind, social and moral improvement, marriage, and criminal behavior.

After 1850 restraint disappeared and verbose men expanded simple essays into bulky books. Only a people mad with success could have endured the length and repetitiousness of these manuals. Many authors simply gathered up their published essays, bound them together, and passed them off as books. In 1871 William Mathews, a Chicago financial writer, published a series of self-help articles in the Chicago *Tribune;* two years later he worked up some new material, added it to his newspaper essays, and marketed the new product under the title *Getting On in the World.* William Maher, a traveling salesman, wrote a series of success essays for the Toledo *Blade,* then republished them as a book, *On the Road to Riches* (1876). Lyman Abbott prepared *How to Succeed* (1882) by culling success snippets from old numbers of *The Christian Union.* Bishop Samuel Fallows put together *The Problem of Success for Young Men and How to Solve It* (1903), using articles which had appeared originally in the Hearst newspapers. Such books had little logical consistency about them and—except to a true believer—must have seemed disorganized and dull.

Many writers, unable to fill whole books from the material in their own heads, cribbed from others. In so doing these latter-day plagiarists simply followed the examples set by Solomon and Franklin. They had no scruples about adapting, quoting, and shamelessly borrowing the words of their own contemporaries. The most casual reading of *How to Do Business* (1857) by the New York phrenologist, Samuel R. Wells, reveals his unacknowledged debts to Edwin T. Freedley's *Practical Treatise on Business* (1852) and Freeman Hunt's *Worth and Wealth* (1856). The strictures against alms houses in A. C. McCurdy's *Win Who Will* (1872) were copied verbatim from *Money for the Million,* a book published in Philadelphia sixteen years before.[19] Since England had an equivalent success cult, American writers also frequently lifted their material from popular English authors. Samuel Smiles was an inexhaustible mine. Other favorite British sources were William Anderson's *Self-Made Men* (1865), John Tulloch's *Beginning Life* (1877), and Frederick William Farrar's *Success in Life* (1885). A reviewer, commenting on Orison Marden's extensive borrowing, observed that "Mr. Marden's labors, of the excerpting and arranging order, must have been something really appalling; and one is glad to reflect that his method was one which relieved him from the additional strain of severe and continuous thought." [20]

Most authors supplemented saws and maxims with anecdotes from the lives of self-made men and sometimes even with full biographical sketches. There were special advantages in the biographical approach, for by the use of specific instances an author could illustrate his points without the repetitious moralizing that was the curse of almost every manual. A few writers allowed the recital of life episodes to speak entirely for themselves. When Charles C. B. Seymour published *Self-Made Men* (1858), setting forth the lives of sixty distinguished men who attained eminence despite humble birth, he boasted that he had not bothered to "append to each sketch a little sermon to point out its moral tendencies." [21] In *The Poor Boy and the Merchant Prince* (1857), William Makepeace Thayer explained the rules of success in terms of the life of Amos Lawrence, but he did not reiterate those rules to the point of boredom. The main object in most sketches was to provide a model for imitation, in the belief that "The biography of every man who has risen to eminence of any kind by his own talent and industry, is a lesson and stimulus to all who read it." [22]

In selecting heroes for emulation, authors had to decide whether they should be statesmen, military leaders, artists, scientists, or businessmen. Before the Civil War businessmen rated second place with professional men and statesmen in the lead. *Men Who Have Risen,* published anonymously in 1859, devoted some space to John Jacob Astor and the Rothschilds, but much more to Elihu Burritt, the linguist, Benjamin West, the artist, Alexander Wilson, the ornithologist, and other professional men. Furthermore, the unidentified author's attitude towards Astor could hardly be considered worshipful. Commenting on the fur trader's middle name, he wrote, "Jacob means a supplanter; that is, one who trips up somebody's heels and takes his place." He also denounced Astor's real estate manipulations on the ground that "The labor of generations yet unborn, the inhabitants of nations yet unknown, is mortgaged in this way to the descendants of John Jacob Astor." On top of everything else, this critic argued that Astor was a skinflint and a liar.[23] After mid-century, as the prestige and power of the business classes increased, politicians and professional men were crowded into the background. Freeman Hunt's two volumes on the *Lives of American Merchants* (1858) set a pattern that was commonly imitated after the Civil War.

The darlings of the self-help cult were Johns Hopkins, George Peabody, Peter Cooper, Ezra Cornell, Amos Lawrence, Elihu Washburne, and others who like them were of good social reputation. When success advisers honored Stephen Girard, John Jacob Astor, Alexander T. Stewart, Cornelius Vanderbilt, and P. T. Barnum, as they sometimes did, they cautioned against imitation of any of their bad qualities. Henry Livingston's *The Money-Maker* (1868) showed how rogues and righteous men made money, but warned that "while we hold up both pictures, we would admonish them to choose the path of honesty and virtue, as the only one of peace and permanent prosperity, both in this life and that which lies beyond it." [24] Matthew H. Smith praised Alexander T. Stewart as a hard-working, persevering, intelligent, and moral man, but balanced his estimate by reporting that Stewart "has probably not a bosom friend in the world" and by describing him as a man of "sharp, cold, avaricious features; a clear, cold eye; a face furrowed with thought, care, and success; a voice harsh and unfriendly in its most mellow tones." [25] Considering the moral foundations of the success cult, concentration on character analysis was almost an obligation. And if only for purposes of contrast, the bad was presented along with the good.

Men who wrote self-help handbooks claimed to be pioneers struggling to create a science of success. If the business world operated on an orderly basis, was it not important to discover the moving principles and record them for the benefit of mankind? Should each generation be required to begin anew on the basis of trial and error? Why not let beginners profit from the hard-won experience of their predecessors? "Would you rather trust to uncertain and dear-bought experience?" asked one adviser. "Would you prefer her slow course? her hard exactions? her bitter fruits? Yes, you *may* learn of her; but you may receive your diploma at too late a day for practical service." [26] When Edwin T. Freedley published a new handbook in 1881 he boasted that hundreds of men had testified to the helpfulness of his earlier volume, *A Practical Treatise on Business* (1852). In his new guide, *The Secret of Success in Life,* he offered his readers the "costly experience of many others, whose names are familiar in the markets and exchanges of the world." [27] Another publicist, William Speer, confidently named his book *The Law of Success* (1885) and proclaimed that even though the science of success was somewhat less exact than mathematics, it was a science none the less and one that any rational man could master. There was sales value in such claims, and perhaps even a nugget of truth, for the manuals summarized a great deal of folksy wisdom, and acquainted the novice with the psychology, if not the methods, of the business community. Their realm was business ethics, not business management. Their scientific principles were nothing other than the moral absolutes of the decalogue. No doubt the popularity of the success cult would have been less had it been scientific in an experimental sense; if it had mass appeal, it was because it preached simple doctrines to simple men.

The Seat of the Scoffers

VIII A SOCIAL IDEA is known through its enemies, no less than through its friends. As a dominant idea in America, self-help had more friends than enemies, but there were many of the latter at both ends of the social scale. On the extreme right the aristocracy of lineage, land, and learning condemned self-help as radical and subversive. On the left it was denounced as the opiate of the people. Such was the fate of a middle-class idea—to be ground between the millstones of reaction and revolution.

The most persistent critics of the success idea spoke as voices from the past, glorifying the serenities of a static agricultural age. They favored an elite that was born, not made, a genteel aristocracy of breeding, manners, and learning. Such critics did not doubt that humble men could rise from rags to riches; rather, they doubted that it was possible for them to rise without subverting the true, the good, and the beautiful. This class of detractors doted on the vulgarity of wealth and constantly affirmed the superiority of non-business values and ways of life. In effect, they asked their fellow men to take up the traditions of a bygone age. Because of its aristocratic bias this line of attack had only a limited appeal. Far from damaging the cult of self-help, it advertised its democratic implications, and by so doing, enhanced its popularity.

Even before the industrial revolution had begun to transform the American economy men who were devoted to agriculture, and to the rural way of life, suspected the motives of the business classes. Thomas Jefferson, who spoke for the small farming interest, thought that merchants sacrificed every honorable principle in order to make money. Merchants, he said, "are least virtuous, and possess the least of the *amor patriae*." In 1818 he complained that under merchant influence Americans were manifesting an enormous greediness for wealth, and declared that from time immemorial this vice had been traceable to the business classes. Since industrialism posed an even greater threat to rural simplicity, independence, and virtue, Jefferson hoped that America could avoid that evil: "for the general operations of manufacture, let our work shops remain in Europe." [1] Other devotees of the rural life shared the same prejudices. James Fenimore Cooper, who spoke for the landed gentry of New York, asserted that merchants invariably pushed their transactions beyond just limits; they responded only to the demands of monetary expediency, ignoring the high principles of natural justice that ought to govern social relations. "A people that deems the possession of riches its highest source of distinction, admits one of the most degrading of all influences to preside over its opinions," Cooper declared.[2] Henry David Thoreau, speaking from a love of rural New England, called attention to the fact that poets and philosophers honored farmers above businessmen: "They have been inclined to regard trade and commerce as not merely uncertain modes of getting a living, but as running into the usurious and disreputable." Thoreau had a brief fling at business himself, working for a time in a pencil factory. But he soon gave it up because he believed it would take at least ten years to get on in that line, and then "I should probably be on my way to the devil." [3] Edgar Allan Poe, who was raised by a Richmond tobacco exporter in whose counting house he worked for a time, preferred the more genteel ways of the South's landed aristocracy. His observations of the business world convinced him that villainy, rather than virtue, held the keys to success. "What the Scriptures mean by the 'leaven of unrighteousness' is that leaven by which men rise," he said.[4]

Many critics of the get-ahead gospel insisted and continued to insist even into the twentieth century that it was impossible to find virtue apart from rural callings and ways of life. As early as 1829 an observer in Philadelphia reported that urban pursuits were rapidly undermining tradtional standards and values. "Away from the busy hum of city life" he said, "in secluded villages and retired hamlets, there may be some pure waters of nature—some hearts uninfluenced by all the absorbing passions of self-interest—but here, in this thronged city, where numberless beings are thronged together in the daily pursuits of life—all are bowing low at the feet of mammon—all are led away from the path of virtue, honor and religion, by that internal curse—'By the sweat of thy brow shalt thou eat bread.' " [5]

Rebecca Harding Davis, a sensitive writer who witnessed the conversion of Pennsylvania from agriculture to industry, insisted that industry sired the mania for money, which in turn subverted the old regard for education, birth, religion, and manners. "In the code of our church-going, Bible-loving ancestors, there was something vulgar, even wicked, in the greed for riches," she declared.[6] Others with rural backgrounds shared the same view. Missouri's Mark Twain, reflecting on the values he had known in his youth, insisted that in his part of the country men knew how to value worth and wealth. "In my youth," he said, "there was nothing resembling a worship of money or of its possessor, in our region. And in our region no well-to-do man was ever charged with having acquired his money by shady methods."[7] But he believed that after the Civil War the robber barons corrupted the old rural definitions of success, and made it impossible to estimate a man's worth by his means. There were moral men of wealth, to be sure, but in the Gilded Age many thoughtful Americans shared the opinion of the governor of New Hampshire, who observed that "A glance over the country will convince the most skeptical that there is a greater proportion of the disciples of James Fisk, the lawless, than of Peter Cooper the philanthropist, in the ranks of the successful."[8]

Critics who spoke in this vein often commented on the distortion of values that accompanied business activity. "If a man walk in the woods for love of them half of each day, he is in danger of being regarded as a loafer," said Thoreau, "but if he spends his whole day as a speculator, shearing off those woods and making earth bald before her time, he is esteemed an industrious and enterprising citizen." As a substitute for the virtue of industry Thoreau proposed the virtue of repose. The busy man had no time for reflection, or for the cultivation of aesthetic and intellectual interests. He was a slave to work, and as such, scarcely a man. "It would be glorious to see mankind at leisure for once," Thoreau declared. "It is nothing but work, work, work. . . . If a man was tossed out of a window when an infant, and so made a cripple for life, or scared out of his wits by the Indians, it is regretted chiefly because he was thus incapacitated for—business! I think there is nothing, not even crime, more opposed to poetry, to philosophy, ay to life itself, than this incessant business." [9] Nor did such sentiments die with Thoreau. In February, 1900, the New Orleans *Picayune,* commenting on the sacrifices required of the successful, asserted that there was much to be said for the social repose of Old World communities where "men still follow their fathers' trades as they take their fathers' names, and where people generally are not working themselves to death in a desperate effort to outshine each other." [10]

Those who criticized self-help in the name of repose were rarely friends of the toiling masses. They represented, instead, the classes that disdained to work with their hands—the landed gentry and the aristocracies of letters and scholarship. Rebecca Harding Davis decried the disease of money-getting, and the businessmen who spread it, but her remedy called only for "a higher class to be imitated, men and women of honest parentage, of gentle breeding and high purposes. . . ." [11] Francis Bellamy, a cousin of Edward Bellamy, denounced self-made rich men in 1903, but not on any socialistic grounds. He charged that self-made men had destroyed the way of life of the older aristocracies—except in New England and the South where "this good fashion of life" lingered on. In New York, he complained, "we see to-day . . . a fashionable society which has no place for statesmen, authors, scientists, editors, unless they are very rich. Newport is still more frank in this rigorous exclusion. The multimillionaire set each summer ignores the naval officers as their ships lie in the harbor. Even President Roosevelt was suffered to visit the place without social recognition; in spite of his high and ancient lineage, he is not rich enough to be in the social swim." [12] Bellamy called for a return to the "serenities of life," and a revival of respect for men of good breeding and culture.

Rarely in this period did men of literary culture try to conceal their scorn of the businessman and his values. Edgar Allan Poe pictured him as a methodical, unimaginative drudge, and a deadly enemy of genius.[13] Oliver Wendell Holmes conceded that it were better to be self-made than not made at all, but confessed that he could not accept the self-made man as the equal of the educated man who had inherited family traditions and the cumulative humanities of several generations. "Above all things," said Holmes, "as a child he should have tumbled about in a library." [14] Nathaniel Hawthorne thought it a pity that Benjamin Franklin's literary reputation in America rested almost entirely on the sayings of Poor Richard, sayings which "are all about getting money or saving it" and which "teach men but a very small portion of their duties." [15] The question of duty also troubled James Russell Lowell, who believed that the sense of duty of a man engaged in commercial affairs did not extend beyond his pocketbook. "Some kind of pace may be got out of the veriest jade by the near prospect of oats," he said; "but the thorough-bred type has the spur in his blood." Lowell was especially disturbed when these upstarts spoke out on social, intellectual, and moral issues; this, as he saw it, was the prerogative of the literary man. He expressed the hope that some day Americans would decide that self-made men had not been "divinely commissioned to fabricate the higher qualities of opinion on all possible topics of human interest." [16]

Educated men were especially resentful of criticism of higher learning. Horace Greeley was their favorite target when, in the years after the Civil War, he went about the country proclaiming that there were few college graduates in the ranks of the business elite. Greeley's critics countered with accounts of their dominance in science, literature, and the professions, where college men won successes which ranked far above the material triumphs achieved in business. And besides, if, as Greeley alleged, there were thousands of unemployed scholars in New York City, this was but a sad commentary on the state of American values. "Let us welcome all genius, grace and learning, as worth more than they can ever bring at the miserable huckster stalls of this world's life," said one friend of higher learning, "and cease to measure the beautiful and grand elements of human nature by the pitiful cheating yardstick of soulless barter." [17] In 1892, after Carnegie had blasted the colleges in the popular press, Winthrop D. Sheldon, an officer of Girard College in Philadelphia, took him to task. Sheldon argued that all learning was valuable, in business and out; that many college men had proved their worth in business; and that if graduates were not millionaires it was because they had refused to become slaves to a tawdry ideal.[18]

Theodore Roosevelt was even more blunt in condemning the views of Andrew Carnegie and Henry Clews on the value of education. Writing for *The Outlook* in 1900 he asserted that neither of these rich men knew what success really was. "Their speeches merely betrayed their own limitations," he said, "and did not furnish any argument against education." Roosevelt approved wealthy men because they "help to upbuild that material national prosperity which must underlie national greatness," but he refused to limit the application of the word success to this one category of men. "Successful statesmen, soldiers, sailors, explorers, historians, poets, and scientific men are also essential to national greatness," he declared, "and, in fact, very much more essential than any mere successful business man can possibly be." [19] Roosevelt also refused to rank businessmen first in prestige. "I am simply unable," he admitted, "to make myself take the attitude of respect toward the very wealthy men which such an enormous multitude of people evidently really feel. I am delighted to show any courtesy to Pierpont Morgan or Andrew Carnegie or James J. Hill, but as far as regarding them as, for instance, I regard Prof. Bury, or Peary, the Arctic explorer, or Rhodes, the historian—why, I could not force myself to do it even if I wanted to, which I don't." [20] Here, in a nutshell, was the artistocratic criticism of the self-help ideal—a dogmatic insistence that self-made men could never be the social equals of men of breeding and culture.

It is doubtful, however, that such assaults weakened the popularity of the success cult with the masses. How many day-laborers enjoyed the serenities of life as they were defined by men of good breeding? How many farmers thought of the rural life as a life of reflection and repose? How many ordinary men favored a society which honored only poets, statesmen, and college graduates? In point of fact, the self-made man was a hero to plain people, their answer to claims that greatness could only be achieved through inheritance. The more conservative critics were also ineffective because they were superficial: they talked vaguely of the immorality of wealth, but deduced immorality from the fact of possession, rather than from a precise analysis of the methods of accumulation. They condemned the self-made man as an enemy of manners and taste but did not inquire whether he was also an enemy of society. They did not argue that the rags-to-riches dream was fallacious, but only that it was unworthy. It was not until more realistic critics began to inquire into the statistical probabilities of success, into the methods of the moneymakers, and into the social origins and consequences of great fortunes, that the success cult suffered any serious damage in the eyes of the masses.

II

One of the fatal weaknesses of the self-help argument was that it explained everything in terms of inner qualities and nothing in terms of the environment. Scientists and social theorists whose vision went beyond the individual found it easy to exploit this weakness. In 1871 Titus M. Coan, a physician who took his cues from Darwin, assaulted the proposition that the causes of success could always be found within the man. His contacts with men of all conditions had convinced him that the successful had no monopoly on ability. Quite to the contrary, he believed abilities were so widely distributed that no one man could stand above his fellows on the basis of talent alone; talented men succeeded only when surrounded by an extraordinary combination of external advantages. Most men, Coan argued, were born in the wrong age or wrong country, "for nature is more wasteful of men than of apple blossoms, and blights a thousand where she ripens one." In each age it was social environment which determined who should succeed and who should fail. The successful were merely the fortunate possessors of talents suited to the times. By the same token, the unsuccessful could not be blamed for failure, because its causes were beyond their control.[21]

Critics knowledgeable in the social sciences were even more scornful of a naïve psychology which argued solely in terms of the individual, ascribing nothing to society. Francis Lieber, the distinguished political scientist, scoffed at the use of such a term as self-made men. "*Self-made men,* indeed!" he once exclaimed to friend, "why don't you tell me of a self-laid egg?" [22] The most thoughtful criticism came from Lester F. Ward, a liberal sociologist. Writing for *The Forum* in 1886, when the worship of success was at its peak, Ward called attention to the fact that self-help advisers completely ignored the operation of social factors in the achievement of success. The necessary personal qualities were abundant, not rare, he argued; if favorable external factors could be correspondingly supplied, many more persons would find success within their reach. "There is no need to search for talent," Ward asserted. "It exists already and everywhere. The thing that is rare is opportunity, not ability." He also rejected as fiction the assertion that struggle against harsh environment was responsible for greatness. "There is no more vicious popular fallacy than that the powers of the mind are strengthened and improved by adversity," he said. "Every one who has accomplished anything, against adverse circumstances, would have accomplished proportionately more had such circumstances been removed." [23] Ward urged that the formula of success could only be made effective by expanding opportunities, that little progress could be made by seeking to cultivate qualities already present in abundance.

By the turn of the century men less astute than Ward had begun to appreciate the relationship between opportunity and success. The rise of the great trusts helped to advertise, as nothing else could, that the average man's chances for success were less than they had been in the pioneering age of business. And a few of the more honest friends of self-help admitted as much. As early as 1885 Andrew Carnegie warned the young men of Pittsburgh that "There is no doubt that it is becoming harder and harder as business gravitates more and more to immense concerns, for a young man without capital to get a start for himself, and in this city especially, where large capital is essential, it is unusually difficult." [24] But like other advisers he insisted that there was still room at the top for boys with the right inner qualities. Orison Marden was even more honest when he wrote in 1903, "In these days of trusts and monopolies, when everything tends to great centres and enormous establishments, when the great fish eat up the little ones, when wealthy men are becoming wealthier, and poor men poorer, one should be extremely cautious about advising young men and young women to go into business with their little, hard-earned savings. . . . Much may be said in favor of working for a salary, especially at a time when the great majority of those who go into business for themselves ultimately go to the wall." [25] Nor was he willing to nourish the myth that wealth awaited those who accepted salaries from the great corporations.

"The fact is that most of us can never hope to be rich," he admitted.[26] Marden and other success advisers began to develop the theme that in an age of combinations success consisted of making the most of limited opportunities. "It is just as much to be a common soldier in the ranks as to be a general that leads," said a handbook published in 1903. "We cannot all be generals. If you are a good soldier in a select crowd, and have a good reputation, that is success in itself." [27]

It is doubtful that such concessions would have been made by defenders of self-help if their lack of realism had not been successfully attacked. Marden, for example, was thoroughly aware of the substantial objections raised by two clergymen of the social gospel school, Bishop Henry C. Potter and Charles H. Parkhurst, the New York municipal reformer. These men insisted that it was foolish to talk of limitless opportunities when, in cities like New York and Chicago, there were ten applicants for every job, and the vast majority were doomed to routine work and meager rewards.[28] "The chances for individual success by the ordinary man . . . are not now so easily seen," said another critic who knew the facts. "The man without special fitness for his task is more likely to remain in the ranks of the toilers than he was a generation ago." [29] What made these claims so damaging was that they could be, and sometimes were, supported with concrete evidence. William James Ghent, a Socialist author, found his evidence in the census returns. Ghent analyzed the statistics on gainful occupations for 1890 and 1900, and discovered that menial jobs in business had increased at a much more rapid rate than executive positions. When he published his findings in *Socialism and Success* (1910) Ghent observed that "Whatever the foregoing figures may be held to indicate regarding 'room at the top,' it is undeniable that they show a generous and growing spaciousness of room at the bottom. They give no warrant for the promise of increased opportunities." His object, as he readily admitted, was to discredit those success advisers who ignored statistical probabilities, who "But one and all . . . neglect to tell you the mathematical and logical chances. Like the agents of a great lottery, they appeal to your gambling instinct; they tell you of the big winning made by Brown or Snigglefritz, and they inspire you to believe that what these men have done you can duplicate. . . . Under even favored conditions . . . not one of you in ten thousand can reasonably hope for a prize." [30] As evidence of this sort piled up in the years after 1900, even the *American Banker,* a thoroughly respectable business journal, decided that the time had come to disavow the rags-to-riches dream. "Yet only a few of us that share the common lot are destined to accumulate great wealth, or achieve conspicuous stations," it warned. "The number of such stations and the chances for such accumulations never did correspond, and never will, to the number of energetic, ambitious and capable men which is hopeful of achieving them. This unpalatable truth the literature of success abhors." [31] Very few business spokesmen were willing to make such sweeping concessions, even in the face of the evidence, but the willingness of the few, and the desperate denials of the many, indicated that the statistical argument against self-help was too damaging to be ignored.

Evidence turned up by twentieth-century scholars indicates that the success cult's critics had all the better of this argument. According to William Miller, only 5 percent of the nation's leading corporation executives in the first decade of this century were men who started as poor boys. And both C. Wright Mills and Pitirim Sorokin discovered through their studies of nineteenth- and twentieth-century business leaders that there were far fewer self-made men in the latter group than in the former.[32] As Ghent and others suspected, after 1890 there was a growing spaciousness of room at the bottom.

III

Even before the statistical improbability of success had been established, critics of self-help had publicized other unpalatable truths about business methods and ethics. In the period between 1880 and 1914 Populists, single-taxers, muckrakers, and Socialists looked behind the moral façade of business to examine the practice. What they found scarcely squared with the wealth-through-virtue theme. Their findings were not entirely new, for skeptics had long suspected that something other than virtue might be involved in the making of money. What was new was the documentation—concrete evidence that the greatest barons were robber barons, men who made their way by corrupting legislatures, appropriating resources, organizing monopolies, and crushing competitors.

Was the rich man's fortune a measure of his contribution to the social welfare? Hardly, said Henry George in *Progress and Poverty* (1879), for if it were, progress and poverty would not go hand in hand. George argued that great fortunes arose out of private monopoly of land, and private appropriation of socially created values in land. Furthermore, he was unwilling to rely on private character to right this wrong; he proposed instead a system of public taxation that would deprive the landlord of that value which he had done nothing to create.[33] Other critics also found that the secret of success lay in the practice of monopoly. In *How to Grow Rich* (1881), Thomas A. Bland, a Southern anti-monopolist who later became a Populist pamphleteer, tried to show that when great fortunes accrued to men it was through their monopoly of both resources and the fruits of other men's labor. His evidence suggested that "in all history, ancient and modern, the examples of men of honest lives and generous hearts who have become rich . . . is so rare as to be exceedingly exceptional, and even these have invariably profited largely . . . by the labor of others." [34] Henry Demarest Lloyd made out the most specific case of all in *Wealth Against Commonwealth* (1894), a detailed study of the dubious methods used to build up the great Standard Oil trust. And Lloyd, like other critics of this school, refused to believe that moral regeneration held the key to a better future. "Our strong men are engaged in a headlong fight for fortune, power, precedence, success," he wrote in 1881. "Americans as they are, they ride over the people like Juggernaut to gain their ends. The moralists have preached to them since the world began, and have failed. The common people, the nation, must take them in hand." [35]

After 1900 those critics whom Theodore Roosevelt denounced as "muckrakers" made their contribution to the evidence and to the indictment. Five years of painstaking work went into Ida M. Tarbell's *History of the Standard Oil Company* (1904), and out of it came proof that rebates, rather than righteousness, provided the foundation for the Rockefeller fortune. Miss Tarbell conceded that Rockefeller was a good man in the sense of private morals, but she concluded that in his business dealings he was unhampered by any ethical considerations. Bouck White's *Book of Daniel Drew* (1910) was even more devastating, because it exposed the moral shifts and evasions by which the notorious cattle-drover, with the aid of the clergy, tried to justify thievery to himself, and himself to the world. Gustavus Myers climaxed the entire muckraking movement with his three-volume *History of the Great American Fortunes* (1910). Myers knew that for decades the moneymakers had "found it to their interest to represent their accumulations as the rewards of industry and ability, and have likewise had the strongest motives for concealing the circumstances of all those complex and devious methods which have been used in building up great fortunes." [36] But like other critics of this school Myers had more faith in records than in rationalizations, and from the records he told a story of the great American fortunes which bore little resemblance to the tales that had come from apostles of self-help. Such revelations were not without effect on public opinion. In 1909 Brander Matthews, a professor of literature at Columbia University, reported that in a very short space of time the attitude of the average man towards the rich had changed completely. Suspicion had replaced awe and respect. "He may at times display too much curiosity about the methods and the amassed money of Mr. Midas and of Mr. Croesus," Matthews observed; "but he does not reveal any too great esteem for their persons. He does not actually envy them, even though he may wish that he also had a little more of the material prosperity of which they have so much." [37]

At this juncture the traditional literature of success seemed puerile and ridiculous when viewed against the muckraker's background of evidence. As a result, self-help handbooks fell under bitter attack. In 1900 Joseph Dana Miller, a founder of the *Single-Tax Review,* furnished the readers of the *Arena* with an analysis of the defects of such literature. Success guides betrayed an utter lack of intellectual discrimination, he said, because many of their assertions were patently false and many more were contradictory. They consisted of hundreds of names and maxims, thrown together in hapazard fashion, and they abounded in irrelevant stories. "But these have to be told, because a book of four hundred and seventy pages must be got together, and one is apt to run short of moral reflections when the attempt is made to give them so large a surface area." [38] But worst of all, in Miller's opinion, these guides encouraged personal qualities that bordered on the anti-social, and they glossed over the hard realities of business practice. On the basis of these failings he considered them more dangerous to young men than the lascivious books that were banned from public libraries. In 1903 the *American Banker* heaped ridicule on the dull heroes of such books, pointing out that "The successful man has never taken a drink, never missed a cue, never told a lie, is never weary, plans and plots incessantly, and probably never sleeps at all. Above all things he always reaches the top and invariably possesses a heavy bank account." [39] Two years later, when Senator Albert J. Beveridge published *The Young Man and the World,* a reviewer for the *Nation* condemned the book on the ground that its author, as a member of the Senate, should have devised a more realistic code of self-help. "The first and great commandment would be to get on," the reviewer said, "and the second would be like unto it, to sacrific everything to that end. If you want money, serve the interests of the corporations which can pay you handsomely. If you have money, debauch the electorate of your State. If you come of good family, comport yourself like a man bred in the gutter. If you have an education, devote yourself to demagoguery. Exert every effort to make politics corrupt and disreputable." But, the reviewer realized, the Senator could not subscribe to this kind of cynicism: "His advice might fitly fall from the lips of any preacher or Sunday-school superintendent in this virtuous land. . . ." [40]

In 1912, after a decade of such assaults, *The Bookman* announced that, owing to the activities of the muckrakers, few publishers would any longer turn out self-help handbooks, and fewer people would buy or read them. "People now like to read the story of a millionaire's success told by some one other than himself. It may be less edifying but it is apt to be more piquant." Viewed in retrospect, it continued, the success literature had never been anything but a humbug, and one that had been overdone. "Lovable as the rich man always is," said *The Bookman,* "we did undoubtedly call him in too often to address the Sunday-school, and let him publish overmuch." [41]

These setbacks which the success cult suffered in the Progressive era were almost, but not quite fatal. Muckrakers, single-taxers, Socialists, and other critics delivered heavy blows but none proved to be lethal. In the twentieth century, as in the nineteenth, faith was more alluring than fact.

My Refuge and My Strength

IX WHAT HAS BEEN the historic function of the self-help idea in America? Who used it, and to what ends? Did it represent the interests of the aspiring poor, or the privileges of the well-to-do? Was it an instrument of social progress, or of reaction and control? If the success ideology is examined in relation to its uses it is apparent that it served many interests and purposes, not just one. On its progressive side it glorified material progress and inspired men to believe that they could enjoy salvation in this life as well as in the next. It encouraged the lowly to defy inherited orders of caste and custom, and to rise as far as their talents would allow. In keeping with the democratic faith it honored activity above repose, and judged merit on the basis of achievement. But on the other side the success gospel inspired material longings that could never be fulfilled, except for a fortunate few. It callously condemned the majority who failed and charged them with delinquency. It reserved the halo of merit for big winners, and suggested, at least indirectly, that success required no explanations and failure permitted no excuses. In America self-help represented both the mighty and the lowly, but it represented them unequally; in time, like men who try to serve two masters, it came to love the one and hate the other, to despise the one and hold to the other.

In the years before the Civil War, when John Jacob Astor, George Peabody, Amos Lawrence and other men of humble beginnings were rising to challenge an older and more genteel aristocracy, the success cult displayed an anti-aristocratic bias. There was a democratic ring in its assurance that every ordinary man could aspire to wealth, and through wealth to the power and prerogatives previously monopolized by the high- and well-born. Public boasting about self-made men represented a challenge to those whose social positions depended upon inheritance rather than accomplishment. Gentlemen did not like to hear popular philosophers assert that "In this country the most prominent and efficient men are not those who were born to wealth and eminent social positions, but those who have won both by the force of untiring personal energy."[1] Nor could they subscribe to Emerson's doctrine that "The mechanic at his bench carries a quiet heart and assured manners, and deals on even terms with men of any condition."[2]

The success cult's glorification of physical labor struck a hard blow at the gentlemanly ideal, which insisted that the superior classes should live without labor. Benjamin Franklin not only worked, but he insisted upon advertising the fact by pushing a wheelbarrow through the streets of Philadelphia in the hope that his creditors would take proper note of his efforts.[3] Franklin's followers, in addition to citing his example, defended the principle on which it was based. "The world is full of fops who never did anything," Ralph Waldo Emerson declared, "and who persuaded beauties and men of genius to wear their fop livery; and these will deliver the fop opinion, that it is not respectable to be seen earning a living; that it is much more respectable to spend without earning. . . . It is the privilege of any human work which is well done to invest the doer with a certain haughtiness. He can well afford not to conciliate, whose faithful work will answer for him."[4] In 1850 Andrew Carnegie had been in America only two years, but it was long enough for him to sense the drift of popular opinion. "It is high time," he observed, "that drones should occupy at least the lowest position in society. A working-man is a more useful citizen and ought to be more respected than an idle prince."[5] Years later he confessed that it was only through a slow process of self-education and self-discipline that he had learned to speak respectfully of those persons who rested their claims to privilege on lineage rather than usefulness.

Since the business world provided some of the newest opportunities for usefulness before the Civil War, it was easy to identify the self-made businessman as a friend of democracy and an enemy of privilege. This was precisely what Henry Clay was doing when he first used the term "self-made men" to identify a class of rising manufacturers who served as symbols of the opportunities of the new industrial age. He wanted to confound Southern leaders who, in defense of their own privileged position, opposed a tariff that promised ordinary men a chance to rise in the industrial sphere. Another business spokesman, Freeman Hunt, sensing that the merchant enjoyed less prestige than the planter, argued that the merchant deserved greater recognition because of his larger services to mankind. "Is not the merchant as respectable a member of the community as the luxurious planter, the time-serving politician, or the cringing office-seeker?" he asked.[6] Before the rise of big business it was not altogether incongruous to identify democracy with industry and commerce. Abraham Lincoln, for example, in accepting the success values of his age, associated them with the economic advance of the common man rather than with the conservative rationale of big business.[7] If the self-help creed had never had any substance in reality, or any connection with the interests of common men, it could scarcely have outlasted the nineteenth century. But it did outlast the century, and the self-made man continued to stand as a symbol of what ordinary men might accomplish under American conditions of opportunity.

To say all this is not to deny that from its infancy the success creed served the interests of the business classes. In the years before the Civil War the noisiest friends of self-help were Northern Whigs, like Edward Everett and Robert C. Winthrop, and the heroes of the cult were not workingmen, but wealthy titans like Stephen Girard and John Jacob Astor. But insofar as success philosophers identified the enemy, the enemy was not labor, it was the aristocracy of inherited privilege. In the first half of the nineteenth century the self-help idea posed a threat to the security of the older privileged classes, and served the interests of a business class that had not yet completed its march to power.

II

In the years after the Civil War when the business class had attained power it used the success rationale to maintain its superiority and consolidate its control. Friends of self-help began to emphasize the inevitability of economic inequality, arguing that even though God provided equal opportunities for all, only a few appreciated and used these gifts. The vast majority, owing to defects of character, squandered their chances and doomed themselves to inferiority. Far from being a new doctrine, this was simply the ancient religious dogma about the saved and the damned, fitted out in secular disguise. It had long been part of the Federalist-Whig social philospohy, and in the eighteenth century had been stated quite clearly by one of the giants of that school, Fisher Ames, when he reasoned, "You have earned an estate; I have not; yet I have a right, and as good a right as another man, to earn it. I may save my earnings and deny myself the pleasures and comforts of life till I have laid up a competent sum to provide for my infirmity and old age. All cannot be rich, but all have a right to make the attempt; and when some have succeeded, and others partially, and others not at all, the several states in which they then find themselves become their condition in life; and whatever the rights of that condition may be, they are to be faithfully secured by the laws and government." [8]

When social convulsions threatened the established order in the period between 1890 and 1917, friends of self-help refurbished these doctrines and used them against levellers. In 1894, in the midst of the Populist uprising, Charles Kendall Adams, president of the University of Wisconsin, warned a class of graduating seniors not to be deceived by the futile efforts of reformers. They could not succeed, he argued, because inequality was rooted in human character, not in society. In the next decade when there was much skepticism about swollen fortunes and the men who amassed them, Bishop William Lawrence came forward with the assertion that it would be easier to suppress the ocean's tide than to prevent a man of acquisitive talents from coming to the top. During the Panic of 1907 Samuel Harden Church, another spokesman for conservative interests, urged a Chautauqua audience to "be practical" about the matter of inequality. "There must always be some men who . . . must occupy subordinate positions," he said. "This law is true in all nature." [9]

Behind such assertions was the conviction that every man was rewarded according to his merit, that luck played no part in the system of distribution. According to success advisers, Dame Fortune was never capricious. "She despises idlers and spendthrifts, abhors knaves and impostors," said a banker who knew his doctrine. "But . . . all who come recommended to her favor, by honesty, prudence, industry and frugality, may confidently hope to be rewarded with her smiles." [10] If luck had nothing to do with success, then bad luck could not be blamed by those who failed. As Henry Ward Beecher once explained, "There are men who, supposing Providence to have an implacable spite against them, bemoan in the poverty of a wretched old age the misfortunes of their lives. Luck forever ran against them, and for others. . . . I never knew an early-rising, hard-working, prudent man, careful of his earnings, and strictly honest, who complained of bad luck. A good character, good habits, and iron industry, are impregnable to the assaults of all the ill luck that fools ever dreamed of." [11] Periodically some heretic in the business community announced that he believed that luck did play a part in success, but defenders of the faith were usually quick to attack his "devouring error," and reassert the merit principle. They had to reply, of course, for if luck could be said to account for the successes of the few, there might be grounds for dispossessing them in the interests of the many. As a trade journal explained to Julius Rosenwald, when he attributed his success to luck, "If financial success were chiefly a matter of luck, there would be strong grounds for the surtaxes that governments so savagely levy on large incomes, for the voraciousness of unionized labor, and for the leveling processes of Socialistic doctrine. This is indeed the very negation of the theory that men get what they earn or earn what they get." [12]

Disgruntled employees were in the habit of attributing their misfortunes to their employers, but this was grossly unfair. According to Edward Bok, Russell Sage, and other notable authorities, employers always advanced their men according to merit, and paid them everything they were capable of earning. Even the most heartless employer, in the interest of efficiency and profits, had to promote and reward his most competent men. Carnegie insisted that the man who complained about the capriciousness of employers was usually the one who had been considered for promotion, but turned down "owing to some objectionable act, habit, or association, of which he thought his employers ignorant." [13]

In times of depression there was a special interest in the merit principle, with success philosophers always trying to explain the plight of the unfortunate in terms of delinquency. In the midst of the Panic of 1873, for example, William Mathews explained distress in Chicago in terms of the extravagance and shortsightedness of the poor. "Instead of hoarding their receipts," he said, "so as to provide against sickness or want of employment, they eat and drink up their earnings as they go, and thus in the first financial crisis, when mills and factories stop, and capitalists lock up their cash instead of using it in great enterprises, they are ruined." [14] During the hard times of 1884–1885 another success expert in Nashville, Tennessee, reported that the fortunate were those who had "regulated their lives by system," while the unfortunate were men who had "either badly managed or not managed at all." [15] In the next decade the president of the University of Wisconsin advised students at that institution to avoid "loose thinking" in regard to the distress brought on by the Panic of 1893. "In a vast number, if not in a majority of cases," said the president, "suffering has come from improvidence, from extravagance, or from dissipation. Let us take care that we do not attribute results to wrong causes." [16] Later the Panic of 1907 caused Lyman Abbott to reflect that employers fired only those men who had failed to make themselves indispensable. "As a rule," said Abbott, "men discharge themselves because they do not make themselves necessary." [17]

Since distress was caused by delinquency it followed that the owners of capital were under no obligation to provide relief through charity. Horace Greeley claimed that one of the calumnies circulated against John Jacob Astor during his lifetime was that he was miserly, but Astor's miserliness, said Greeley, was his only defense against "the incessant beggary and importunity of those who have nothing, and do not mean to earn anything." [18] Greeley doubted that half the population did not know how the other half lived; his theory was that each half knew very well, because the beggar half lived off the industrious half, or at least tried to do so. Other friends of self-help thought that alms houses should be abolished, and that missionaries should be sent to tell these "home heathen" that it was a law of God that those who do not work shall not eat. One extremist advocated the systematic starvation of paupers, on the ground that they had deliberately chosen a life of poverty, and deserved to suffer the just and natural penalties of their choice.[19]

If every man reaped rewards according to his merit what need was there for trade unions? Trade unions penalized the industrious, protected the inefficient, and tried to coerce employers into granting rewards that labor had not earned. Unions also attempted the impossible because they tried to put all their members on an equal financial footing. This was a terrible error for, as Bishop Samuel Fallows explained, "No . . . labor organization can make, by any political economy known to man, the slow-going tortoise travel as fast as the swift-footed hare in the financial race." [20] Men who joined unions and engaged in strikes damaged their own prospects, for under the theory of identical interests anything that hurt the employer also hurt the worker. The wise employee tried to advance his master's interests, and thereby advanced his own. As Lyman Abbott observed, "If half the energy put into getting more wages and cutting down hours were put into cheerful, faithful, competent work, far more would be accomplished in the way of securing better conditions." [21]

The same principle applied with even greater force to radical political activity and projects aiming at social revolution. Before the Civil War friends of self-help were untroubled by the fear of social revolution, and they rarely preached against it. In 1841 Governor Edward Everett of Massachusetts declared that so long as the wheel of fortune continued to revolve, holding out the hope that the poor of one generation would become the rich of the next, there was no need to fear revolution. What man would be so foolish as to make war on the prospects of his children?[22] In the same year William Ellery Channing observed that there was much unrest in the land, but he rejoiced that the unrest was caused by men trying to make money. "Of all the dreams of fear," he said, "few seem to me more baseless than the dream of anarchy among a people who are possessed almost to a man with the passion for gain."[23] Matthew H. Smith, reflecting on the European revolutions of 1848, concluded that such disturbances would never have occurred if Europeans had enjoyed the same moneymaking opportunities as Americans.[24] Even after the turn of the twentieth century, when there was greater alarm on this point, Andrew Carnegie assured the plutocracy that there was nothing to fear since the working classes were still enchanted by the expectation of recognition, advancement, and wealth.[25] But in this, as in much else, Carnegie was more optimistic than most conservatives.

Fear of social convulsion increased after 1890, and conservative spokesmen consciously preached self-help as an antidote to radicalism. Grover Cleveland, his faith shaken by Bryan and the free-silver agitation of 1896, told a Princeton audience in the following year that self-made men must enter politics as never before "for what they may do in patriotically steadying the currents of political sentiment and action." He anticipated that self-made men would counteract the influence of "the lying partisan and flattering demagogue," and make the mass of voters more responsible. That land was fortunate where the people ruled, said Cleveland, but that land was more fortunate where the people's government was "controlled, watched and defended by the virtue, patriotism, and intelligence of truly self-made men." [26] The upsurge of Socialist sentiment after 1900 led conservatives to invoke memories of self-made men who had solved their problems not by rebellion but by the cultivation of the economic virtues. In 1914, when corporation lawyer James L. Beck unveiled a statue to Franklin in Philadelphia, he urged his audience to cultivate Franklin's virtues, and re-study his maxims, by way of insulating themselves against the radicalism of the age. He also expressed the hope that Franklin's memory would live forever as a symbol of self-reliance in the face of uncertainty, and that every American would "pray God that the darkening clouds of socialism and even anarchy are not in our day to obscure this beneficent luminary of civilization." [27] One of the commonplaces of this school was that workingmen had more to gain from honest industry than from vague projects of social regeneration.

In the period after 1890 the self-help argument was used more and more to attack Populism, Socialism, and Progressivism. The enmity was natural, of course, because each of those movements attempted to redress grievances by reforming society, not by reforming individuals. But in resisting programs framed for the common man, conservatives helped to advertise the fact that in the twentieth century the success argument was much more useful as an instrument of social control than as an instrument of social progress.

III

In addition to attacking every form of radicalism friends of self-help actively defended the motives and methods of the rich. This defense was especially necessary after 1890 when millionaires were so generally misunderstood and so little appreciated. Who knew what libels and calumnies the wealthy businessman suffered? Who appreciated his genuine sympathy for the unfortunate classes, his sleepless nights given over to the planning of new and useful enterprises, his worries over the responsibilities of stewardship? Most men pitied the poor and despised the rich, but only because they did not understand that the poor lived without care, while the rich carried the burdens of mankind. "As a rule," said Andrew Carnegie, "there is more genuine satisfaction, a truer life, and more obtained from life in the humble cottages of the poor than in the palaces of the rich." [28] It was this theme, as much as anything else, that made Elbert Hubbard's *A Message to Garcia* so popular in the business community:

> We have recently been hearing much maudlin sympathy expressed for the "downtrodden denizens of the sweatshop" and the "homeless wanderer searching for honest employment," and with it all often go many hard words for the men in power. Nothing is said about the employer who grows old before his time in a vain attempt to get frowsy ne'er do wells to do intelligent work; and his long, patient striving after "help" that does nothing but loaf when his back is turned . . . in our pitying let us drop a tear, too, for the men who are striving to carry on a great enterprise, whose working hours are not limited by the whistle, and whose hair is fast turning white through the struggle to hold in line dowdy indifference, slipshod imbecility, and the heartless ingratitude which, but for their enterprise, would be both hungry and homeless . . . when all the world has gone a-slumming I wish to speak a word of sympathy for the man who succeeds—the man who, against

> great odds, has directed the efforts of others, and having succeeded, finds there's nothing in it: nothing but bare boards and clothes.[29]

Whenever rich men were attacked, as they often were in the Progressive era, they or their friends put up defenses on this line.

Business barons boasted that they were agents of progress. But what of Henry George's charge that progress and poverty go hand in hand? Andrew Carnegie answered that one himself. "So far as I have observed," he said, "all writers of authority upon social and economic subjects have not only disputed Mr. George's statements, but pronounce their opposites to be the truth." Compare the least progressive nations with the most progressive, he urged. Which have the millionaires, and which have not? What is the condition of the masses in China, India, and Russia? What is it in the United States and Great Britain? "In a country where the millionaire exists there is little excuse for pauperism," he declared; "the condition of the masses is satisfactory just in proportion as a country is blessed with millionaires." [30] Those who understood the ways of the businessman agreed with this analysis. In 1901 Bishop William Lawrence, for example, assured his fellow Americans that the nation's industrial leaders were putting an end to poverty, ignorance, disease, and even aesthetic barrenness.[31] And in 1907 a professor of mechanical engineering at Cornell University was even more lavish in his praise, declaring that "the noblest work of all, in our time or in times to come, shall be adjudged that of the captain of industry, who, in his long life of struggle and of strife . . . finds employment for thousands, gives the people some essential of the people's life at continually rising wages, gathers his millions while giving to the nation hundreds of millions, and then his struggles and strifes at an end, gives his remaining years to distribution of his wealth in the founding of libraries and to the support of the higher education that he himself may lack." [32] From the pulpit, the rostrum, and the pages of the leading conservative journals came endless assurances that wealthy self-made men were not robber barons, but the noblest of benefactors.

If we may judge by their utterances during the first decade of this century, the charge that troubled the great barons most was the charge that they had restricted and destroyed opportunities. Optimists in the nineteenth century, and self-made men most of all, had taken opportunity for granted. But men who came to maturity in the early twentieth century were less sanguine about their prospects. Where was the new frontier? Where were the fresh supplies of timber, and deposits of coal and oil? Where was the world of small business that the giants had known in their youth? In the Progressive era these questions had to be answered in courts of law, and before the bar of public opinion. There were a few like Carnegie who admitted that their fortunes had been carved out of a new and undeveloped continent, and under conditions that no longer existed. But the vast majority tried to maintain the fiction that opportunities were the same yesterday, today, and forever more. In an age of trusts every man could still make of himself whatever he chose, there was always a market for personal wares, the combines appreciated energy and enterprise, and every success was possible.

Russell Sage recalled that in his youth no one complained of lacking opportunity: the trouble with young men in the twentieth century was that they lacked the grit and will to succeed. Others claimed the younger generation did not want to work. William H. Kimball, president of the Seventh National Bank of New York, asserted that "The outcry that the trusts are taking away the opportunities of young men affords a good excuse for those who do not wish to work." [33] Friends of the business community alleged that the problem was not to find work for men, but rather to find men for work. Corporations provided abundant opportunities, said Edward Bok, but "the average young man of today is incapable of filling them, or if he be not exactly incapable . . . he is unwilling, which is even worse." [34] Only those who searched for able, ambitious men knew how difficult it was to find them, and how little most men appreciated opportunities even when they were offered. To be sure, there were many complaints about insufficient chances, but the answer to this was that "All occupations and avenues of endeavor are overcrowded to the indolent, the nerveless and the incompetent." [35] Francis V. Greene, an asphalt and power magnate, argued that only the most competent suffered under the combines because they had to settle for large salaries instead of large fortunes. The half-competent did not suffer; instead they benefitted in that they were saved from entering business on their own, only to fail. And last but not least, the trusts permitted the incompetent to "sit on the park benches as they would have done before." [36] When Elbert H. Gary of the United States Steel Corporation was called to testify he fell back on the cliché that "as always, everywhere, in every line and department of human activity, there is an abundance of room at the top." [37] Charles M. Schwab asserted that it was a terrible mistake to think that all the great fortunes had been made; more would be made in the future, because ambitious Americans would do as they had always done—make their own opportunities. Louis M. Stern, one of the nation's leading dry goods merchants, insisted that the idea that chances were limited was "nothing but talk." [38]

The most precious testimony came from John D. Rockefeller in the year 1907. At the time the oil king was something of an interested party, since there was an anti-trust suit pending against the Standard Oil Company in the federal courts. The combines, he said, had expanded rather than limited opportunity. Within his own company, he declared, there was a steady progression from office-boy to executive, and this was only a reflection of what was happening everywhere, for the demand for able young men far exceeded the supply. Throughout the industrial system apprentices were becoming master-workmen; master-workmen were becoming superintendents; superintendents were becoming executives. "It is a constant procession," Rockefeller observed. "At the forge and in the counting room to-day are the young men who ten, twenty years hence will be the captains of industry of their day." The child of the tenement and the barefoot country boy had no cause for despair. "I see in each of them infinite possibilities," he said. "They have but to master the knack of economy, thrift, honesty, and perseverance, and success is theirs." [39] Exactly twenty years later another authority talked to the officers of the Standard Oil Company about character and honesty as keys to business success. He did not mention parentage, though he might have, for his name was John D. Rockefeller, Jr.[40]

As long as the anti-trust drive continued, friends of the combines took refuge in the self-help argument. In 1916

The Commercial and Financial Chronicle attacked the Federal Trade Commission on the ground that it was trying to push small businessmen and other inefficient persons up the ladder to success. The *Chronicle* believed the Commission's efforts were misguided, for "the individual must achieve his own climb to success." Besides, the Commission was trying to "coddle the slow, instead of bidding him raise his head and use his own powers." As this respectable financial paper saw it the whole American tradition of success was being undermined by governmental restrictions "either actual, promised, talked of or feared." [41] There was something to the charge. In the nineteenth century self-made men had not had to pay taxes on personal incomes, they had enjoyed easy access to the public domain, and for the most part they had been unhampered by public regulation. On the eve of the first World War men could still make money, but only under handicaps. Business critics blamed the trusts, the friends of the trusts blamed an unfriendly government. Quite apart from the question of blame, however, one fact stood out: the American self-help tradition had fallen upon evil days.

Epilogue

CRITICS WHO ANTICIPATED the success cult's final demise in the years from 1900 to 1915 were more than a little premature. They had confused a serious illness with a fatal one, and ignored the curative powers of prosperity. As business reached a higher level of activity in the period from 1915 to 1929 the worship of success was revitalized and ancient truths were reestablished in the hearts of the people.

Of course the new cult was not exactly the same as the old. The old high priests, Orison Marden and Edward Bok, resigned in favor of Bruce Barton and Roger W. Babson, younger men who knew the spirit of the times, who knew that the day had passed when simple country boys could become sole owners of large enterprises. With chances for success controlled by the corporations and by the widows and orphans who owned them, the trick now was to rise into the managerial elite. The problem, as Bruce Barton phrased it for the *American Mercury* in 1922, was to know "What to Do if You Want to Sit at the Boss's Desk." This was a worthy ambition as far as it went, but it was not the same aspiration which had excited self-made men fifty years before. Andrew Carnegie, for instance, had always thought ill of the man who did not aspire to own his own business and to be his own boss. To his way of thinking the salaried executive was only an underling who did not deserve to be ranked with independent men. In contrast the success cult's glorification of hired managers during the 1920's represented at the very least a retreat from the traditional ideal of independence.

There was retreat on other fronts too. Continuing a trend inaugurated at the turn of the century, success advisers urged young men to get as much schooling as possible. "The self-made manager in business is nearing the end of his road," one of them reported in 1924. "He cannot escape the relentless pursuit of the same forces that have eliminated self-made lawyers and doctors and admirals. Despite his own blind faith in the 'practical,' he is already hiring professionally trained engineers, chemists, accountants, and hygienists. He is more and more dependent upon them, and he knows it. He must himself turn to professional education, or surrender control to those who do." [1] In a sense it was true that the young man who made his way into the managerial elite after working his way through college was a self-made man, but who could mistake him for Cornelius Vanderbilt or John Jacob Astor?

Other changes in attitude toward success indicated adjustment to the postwar world. The more sophisticated counselors, alive to a popular interest in psychology, talked less about improvement of character and more about improvement of personality. The science of the hour was the science of "human engineering." The man who wanted to get ahead had to learn how to get along with others, how to conquer self-created fear, and how to develop personal efficiency. To help him, popular journals published "Questions That Will Help You Get a Line on Yourself," and weighty articles on "Intelligence, Interest, and Energy," and the art of "Putting Your Best Foot Forward." A generation that scoffed at the phrenologist's pretense of reading vocations by the external contours of the head delivered itself into the hands of vocational guidance experts who, armed with the new intelligence and aptitude tests, proposed the more mysterious feat of reading vocations by the internal contours of the mind.

Despite these variations on the success theme, doctrine remained fundamentally the same. The secret of success still had to be found in the man rather than in the society, and in cultivated rather than in inherited qualities. Genius counted for as little in the 1920s as in the middle of the nineteenth century. In 1924 an author for the *American Mercury* explained "Why I Never Hire Brilliant Men," and five years later, at the time of the great Wall Street crash, Bruce Barton asserted that "It is, I believe, the most completely provable fact in business that brilliance is more likely to be a curse than an asset, and that a hard-hitting mediocrity is almost certain to score over genius." [2] Business publicists still argued that the difference between the man who earned a hundred thousand a year and the man who earned a thousand was not a difference in natural endowment, but a difference in willpower, perseverance, ambition, and industry. Times had changed, but when it came to explaining the gulf that separated the rich from the poor the economic virtues still had their uses and their champions.

The champions also had a familiar look, for they represented the traditional synthesis of religion, business, and journalism. Roger W. Babson, the son of a Gloucester, Massachusetts, dry goods merchant, came directly out of the Puritan religious tradition, like many of the proph-

ets of old. A Congregationalist by faith, he had as much interest in religion as in business, and in his published works, such as *Religion and Business* (1920), he expounded the relation between the two. Bruce Barton, whose interests also embraced the spiritual and the material, was not a Yankee, but he was a minister's son, and like Babson, a Congregationalist. His best-selling book, *The Man Nobody Knows* (1925), portrayed Jesus as an aggressive type of modern businessman, a dynamic organizer and advertiser. Barton, himself, had some success in this respect, for he eventually became chairman of the board of Batten, Barton, Durstine, and Osborn, a leading New York advertising firm. Priests such as these helped take the sharp edge of materialism off the gospel of success but they did not alter its nature, which was the same in their day as in that of Benjamin Franklin. Success, defined in terms of money lost little luster with age. "Obviously," said an observer of the American scene in the twenties, "the poor would like to get rich, and the rich would like to roll in more riches." [3]

After 1929, thanks to the great depression, this was easier to say than to do. As virtuous men took their places in the breadlines, silence fell over many of the sages who had vouched for the doctrine of wealth through virtue. Slick magazines printed fewer articles on how to climb the executive ladder, and more on how to make the best of failure. Periodically some journal called attention to a career which proved that "It Still Happens in America," but there was a defensive note in such efforts. Not everybody, however, assumed this defensive posture. Babson, for example, having forecast the coming of the depression, stood his ground when it came, insisting that it was absurd to blame the crisis on events in Europe, or on the

President, or on any other factor beyond the control of the individual. What the business world lacked, he said, was men of spiritual power, the kind of men who first made America.[4] The secret of recovery lay not in social experimentation, but in the regeneration of the individual. "Hard work, hard thinking, efficiency and integrity are coming back into vogue," he declared in 1932. "The surest signal of business recovery is the recovery that is already taking place in our ideals." [5]

That final recovery from the depression depended upon the recovery of time-tested ideals, particularly the ideal of self-help, is highly debatable. For one thing, there is no proof that the ideal was ever lost. In the interest of logical consistency philosophers who attributed prosperity to private economic virtue may have found it necessary to attribute depression to lack of it, but the attribution does not make it so. The doctrine that men prospered in one decade because they were virtuous, and suffered in the next because they were not, puts credulity to the test. It also reveals the hopeless inadequacy of that method of social analysis which rests upon moral clichés.

Enthusiasm for the gospel of wealth fell off somewhat after 1929, but this was a consequence of the depression, not a cause. Since this gospel had always fed on opportunity, the decline of opportunity was bound to raise doubts among the faithful. The surprise of these gloomy years is not that this material religion lost some of its enchantment, but that it did not lose it altogether. Ordinary men never had fewer chances, yet they kept alive an expectancy of better days to come and clung to the fundamentals of the faith. When sociologist Robert S. Lynd revisited Muncie, Indiana, in the mid-thirties, he discovered that the community's social faith, though somewhat shaken, was still intact. The money definition of success still obtained, and men believed that in the future Americans would have every opportunity to win as much material success as their characters and talents would allow.[6] Numerous public opinion polls, taken after the return of prosperity, confirmed this optimistic state of mind. Both during and after World War II Americans were confident that chances for the next generation would be at least as good as they had been in the past and probably better. In the higher realms of faith there was plenty of room at the top.[7]

Scholars, meantime, were busy at the task of setting the record straight. In recent years sociologists, business historians, and others have piled up mountains of impressive statistical data to prove conclusively that a majority of our wealthy citizens do not now, and never did, come up from the ranks of the poor. Through all our history the self-made man was the exception not the rule. American opportunities have been magnificent, but they have never equalled the aspirations of the whole people; success has been for the few, not the many. These are the facts, but do men order their lives according to fact alone? Men who occupy the lowest places in our society have known the facts for a long time, by living with them from day to day. But they are not content with facts, for facts are dull companions, and dangerous besides. Men on the bottom need dreams, and over the years Edward Bok, Orison Marden, Russell Conwell and other philosophers of our business civilization have been only too happy to supply them. Belief in the self-made man requires only an act of faith, and, as every Sunday School boy knows, faith is simply the substance of things hoped for, the evidence of things not seen.

Notes

CHAPTER I.

[1] James A. Garfield, *Elements of Success* (Washington, 1881), p. 6. For popular accounts of Garfield's rise, see William M. Thayer, *From Log-Cabin to the White House* (Boston, 1881), and Horatio Alger, *From Canal Boy to President* (New York, 1881).

[2] "Success in Life," *Harper's New Monthly Magazine,* VII (1853), 238.

[3] Frederick W. Farrar, *Success in Life* (Boston, 1885), p. 21.

[4] William A. Craigie and James R. Hulbert, eds., *A Dictionary of American English* (4 vols., Chicago, 1944), IV, 2065; *Register of Debates in Congress* (14 vols., Washington, 1825–37), VIII, Part 1, 277.

[5] For a discussion of social promotion under European conditions, consult Pitirim Sorokin, *Social Mobility* (New York, 1927), pp. 139, 164–183.

[6] Louis B. Wright analyzes English success literature in *Middle Class Culture in Elizabethan England* (Chapel Hill, 1935), pp. 165–200.

[7] Ralph Barton Perry, *Puritanism and Democracy* (New York, 1944), p. 298. See also Arthur M. Schlesinger, "What Then Is the American, This New Man?" *American Historical Review,* XLVIII (1943), 227, 237, 239.

[8] Quoted in T. J. Wertenbaker, *The Golden Age of Colonial Culture* (New York, 1942), p. 48.

[9] The best analysis of Cotton Mather's ideas on business success is in Alfred W. Griswold, "Three Puritans on Prosperity," *New England Quarterly,* VII (1934), 475–493.

[10] For Franklin's influence on the nineteenth-century success ideology, see Louis B. Wright, "Franklin's Legacy to the Gilded Age," *Virginia Quarterly Review,* XXII (1946), 268–279.

[11] Simeon Ide, ed., *Benjamin Franklin, The Way to Wealth, Advice to Young Tradesmen, and Sketches of His Life and Character* (Windsor, Vt., 1826), p. 39.

[12] Edward Everett, *Orations and Speeches on Various Occasions by Edward Everett* (Boston, 1836), pp. 298–299.

[13] Robert C. Winthrop, *Oration at the Inauguration of the Statue of Benjamin Franklin* (Boston, 1856), p. 25.

[14] Quoted in Harvey O'Connor, *Mellon's Millions* (New York, 1933), p. 4.

[15] Sorokin, "American Millionaires and Multi-Millionaires," *Journal of Social Forces,* III (1925), 634, 639. See also C. Wright Mills, "The American Business Elite: a Collective Portrait," *The Tasks of Economic History,* Supplement V (1945), 22.

[16] William Ellery Channing, "The Present Age," in *The Works of William Ellery Channing* (Boston, 1887), p. 165. Channing delivered this address to the Mercantile Library Company of Philadelphia, May 11, 1841.

[17] Ralph Waldo Emerson, *The Conduct of Life* (Boston, 1904), p. 95.

[18] Oliver Wendell Holmes, *The Autocrat of the Breakfast Table* (Boston, 1892), p. 259.

[19] John Aiken, *Labor and Wages, at Home and Abroad* (Lowell, 1849), p. 16.

[20] Moses Y. Beach, *Wealth and Pedigree of the Wealthy Citizens of New York City* (4th ed., New York, 1842), p. 3. According to a later estimate New York City boasted twenty millionaires in 1855, most of whom had earned their fortunes in commerce and real estate. See Robert G. Albion, *The Rise of New York Port* (New York, 1939), p. 259.

[21] Beach, *Wealth and Pedigree* (4th ed.), p. 2; *Ibid.* (11th ed., New York, 1846), p. 1.

[22] Quoted in Freeman Hunt, *Worth and Wealth* (New York, 1856), pp. 350–351. Arthur's best known success handbook was *Advice to Young Men on Their Duties and Conduct in Life* (Boston, 1848).

[23] William H. Van Doren, *Mercantile Morals* (New York, 1852), p. 103.

CHAPTER II.

[1] Phineas T. Barnum, *The Art of Money-Getting* (New York, 1882), p. 7.

[2] Robert W. Cushman, *Elements of Success* (Washington, 1848), p. 10.

[3] A. C. McCurdy, *Win Who Will* (Philadelphia, 1872), p. 19. See also *Money for the Million* (Philadelphia, 1856), pp. ix–x; W. T. Hamilton, *The Responsibilities of American Youth* (Mobile, 1851), p. 12.

[4] Horace Greeley, *Success in Business* (New York, 1867), p. 16. See also Charles H. Bell, "The Worship of Success," in Clark S. Northup, ed., *Representative Phi Beta Kappa Orations* (Boston, 1915), p. 175.

[5] Orison S. Marden, *The Young Man Entering Business* (New York, 1903), p. 206.

[6] Quoted in Edna Dean Proctor, ed., *Life Thoughts* (Boston, 1859), p. 299. Horace Mann once denounced inherited wealth as "a sort of human oyster bed, where heirs and heiresses are planted, to spend a contemptible life of slothfulness in growing plump and succulent for the grave-worm's banquet." Horace Mann, *A Few Thoughts for a Young Man* (Boston, 1887), pp. 45–46.

[7] Andrew Carnegie, *The Gospel of Wealth* (New York, 1900), p. 64.

[8] Carnegie, *The Empire of Business* (New York, 1902), p. 129.

[9] Sorokin, "American Millionaires," *Journal of Social Forces,* III (1925), 636; Mills, "Business Elite," *Tasks of Economic History,* Supplement V (1945), 30, 42, 44. Only 5 percent of the top business leaders active in the first decade of the twentieth century originated in the lower classes. See William Miller, "American Historians and the Business Elite," *Journal of Economic History,* IX (1949), 206.

[10] Marden, *Pushing to the Front* (Toledo, 1911), p. 53.

[11] Albion, *Rise of New York Port,* pp. 240–244. Of the distinguished businessmen listed in the *Dictionary of American*

Biography, 32 percent were New Englanders, but only 22 percent won their successes in New England. The Middle Atlantic states, contributing 29 percent of the elite, served as the locale in which 39 percent of the leaders achieved distinction. See Mills, "Business Elite," *Tasks of Economic History,* Supplement V (1945), 22.

[12] Joseph A. Scoville, *The Old Merchants of New York City* (3 vols., New York, 1870), I, 56.

[13] *Ibid.,* I, 57, 194–195; II, 101–102.

[14] Wilbur F. Crafts, *Successful Men of Today and What They Say of Success* (New York, 1883), pp. 16–17.

[15] W. J. Spillman, "The Country Boy," *Science,* XXX (1909), 406.

[16] Sorokin, "American Millionaires," *Journal of Social Forces,* III (1925), 635; Mills, "Business Elite," *Tasks of Economic History,* Supplement V (1945), 32; Miller, "American Historians and the Business Elite," *Journal of Economic History,* IX (1949), 204.

[17] Crafts, *Successful Men,* p. 17. See also Thomas L. Haines and L. W. Yaggy, *The Royal Path of Life* (Chicago, 1879), pp. 234–235; Matthew H. Smith, "The Elements of Business Success," *Hunt's Merchants' Magazine,* XXXI (1854), 57–58.

[18] Quoted in Spillman, "Country Boy," *Science,* XXX (1909), 407.

[19] Matthew H. Smith, *Successful Folks* (Hartford, 1878), p. 204.

[20] H. L. Reade, *Success in Business* (Hartford, 1875), p. 68. See also *The Problem of Success for Young Men and How to Solve It* (New York, 1903), p. 168; Barnum, *Money-Getting,* p. 23.

[21] Marden, *Pushing to the Front,* p. 725.

[22] Albert J. Beveridge, *The Young Man and the World* (New York, 1928), p. 56.

[23] Quoted in Elbert Hubbard, *Little Journeys to the Homes of the Great* (14 vols., New York, 1928), XI, 171. For other tributes to mothers see Carnegie, *Autobiography of Andrew Carnegie* (Boston, 1920), pp. 6, 31; Marden, *Pushing to the Front,* pp. 725–738; Haines and Yaggy, *Royal Path of Life,* pp. 29–57.

[24] Edward Bok, "The Young Man in Business," *Cosmopolitan,* XVI (1894), 339; *Money for the Million,* p. 74; Louisa C. Tuthill, *The Merchant* (New York, 1850), pp. 150–158; Crafts, *Successful Men,* p. 24; Beveridge, *Young Man,* p. 162.

[25] George C. Eggleston, *How to Make a Living* (New York, 1875), p. 41.

[26] John Frost, *The Young Merchant* (Boston, 1841), p. 117.

[27] Charles M. Schwab, *Succeeding With What You Have* (New York, 1917), pp. 60–61.

[28] Tuthill, *The Merchant,* p. 155.

[29] Sorokin, "American Millionaires," *Journal of Social Forces,* III (1925), 629.

[30] Eggleston, *How to Make a Living,* p. 40.

[31] Ralph Waldo Emerson, *The Complete Works of Ralph Waldo Emerson* (12 vols., Boston, 1903–04), III, 92. In his essay on wealth Emerson wrote, "There is always a reason, *in the man,* for his good or bad fortune, and so in making money." *Ibid.,* VI, 100.

[32] Quoted in Ralph Waldo Trine, *The Power That Wins* (Indianapolis, 1929), p. 62.

[33] Frank Greene, "Business Success and Failure," *Century Magazine,* LXXIX (1910), 585. Dun and Bradstreet computed failures not in terms of the number of persons who failed, but rather in terms of the proportion of money lost owing to various causes. Thus, according to Dun and Bradstreet figures, 22 percent of all money lost in the eight years preceding 1910 was lost because of personal incompetence, 10 percent because of fraud, 6 percent because of inexperience, 6 percent because of neglect and unwise credits, and 2 percent because of extravagance and speculation. For an explanation of this method of computing losses, see "Business Failures," *Annals of the American Academy,* XVII (1901), 213.

CHAPTER III.

[1] Theodore Roosevelt, "Character and Success," *Outlook,* LXIV (1900), 725.

[2] As late as 1896 there were fewer than a dozen American corporations, railroads excepted, capitalized at ten million dollars or more. See Miller, "American Historians and the Business

Elite," *Journal of Economic History,* IX (1949), 188. A more extended discussion of the relation of corporations to individual opportunity runs through later chapters of this study.

[3] Henry Ward Beecher, *Seven Lectures to Young Men* (Indianapolis, 1844), pp. 16–17. On Beecher's dullness, see William Dale Owen, *Success in Life* (Chicago, 1878), p. 21.

[4] James D. Mills, *The Art of Money Making* (New York, 1872), p. 188.

[5] Theodore Parker, *The Works of Theodore Parker* (15 vols., Boston, 1907–13), V, 111.

[6] Marden, *Entering Business,* p. 27. See also William H. Maher, *On the Road to Riches* (Toledo, 1876), p. 10; John Tulloch, *Beginning Life* (New York, 1877), pp. 198–199; Frank Fergurson, *The Young Man* (Boston, 1848), pp. 58–59.

[7] Marden, *Entering Business,* p. 142. See also H. L. Reade, *Money, and How to Make It* (Norwich, Conn., 1872), p. 415; Adam Craig, ed., *Room at the Top* (Chicago, 1883), p. 29; Charles P. Masden, *The Sacredness of Business* (Milwaukee, 1898), p. 7.

[8] William Mathews, *Getting on in the World* (Chicago, 1874), p. 280.

[9] Barnum, *Money-Getting,* pp. 22–23.

[10] Joseph Simms, *The Secrets of Success in Life* (London, 1873), p. 1.

[11] Owen, *Success in Life,* p. 471. See also Titus M. Coan, "Successful People," *Galaxy,* XI (1871), 221; Edward Bok, *The Keys to Success* (Philadelphia, 1898), p. 99; William Lawrence, *The Elements of Success* (Cincinnati, 1873), p. 4.

[12] Carnegie, *Empire of Business,* p. 83.

[13] Owen, *Success in Life,* p. 345.

[14] *Money for the Million,* p. 58. For further discussion of the relation of willpower to success, see William A. Alcott, *The Young Man's Guide* (Boston, 1841), p. 29; M. B. Stewart, "Self-Made," *The Ladies' Repository,* XIX (1859), 485–486; Tulloch, *Beginning Life,* p. 198; Carnegie, *Gospel of Wealth,* p. 64.

[15] Alcott, *Young Man's Guide,* pp. 48–49. For a more comprehensive treatment of the economic virtues, consult Donald W.

McConnell, *Economic Virtues in the United States* (New York, 1930).

[16] John Tulloch, quoted in Craig, ed., *Room at the Top,* p. 18.

[17] Arthur, *Advice to Young Men,* p. 82. On the evils of idleness, see Daniel Wise, *The Young Man's Counsellor* (New York, 1854), pp. 90–91; E. F. Dagley, "The Industry of Idleness," in *The American Juvenile Keepsake* (New York, 1834), p. 116.

[18] Alcott, *Young Man's Guide,* pp. 38–39.

[19] "Idleness," in *Appleton's Juvenile Annual for 1871* (New York, 1871), p. 169.

[20] Simms, *Secrets of Success,* p. 6.

[21] A. Hall, *A Manual of Morals for Common Schools* (Boston, 1849), p. 90.

[22] Crafts, *Successful Men,* p. 26. Not all the leaders represented in this survey were businessmen. A professional man, President Andrew Dixon White of Cornell University, told Crafts that he had never engaged in physical labor in his youth. "I consider this as a matter of regret," White said. *Ibid.,* p. 226.

[23] *The Problem of Success for Young Men and How to Solve It* (New York, 1903), p. 73. This volume consists of a collection of essays written by prominent men for the Hearst newspapers.

[24] Quoted in Frank W. Taussig and C. S. Joslyn, *American Business Leaders* (New York, 1932), pp. 299–301.

[25] Report of W. P. Groser, in A. Mosely, *Reports of the Mosely Educational Commission to the United States of America, October–December, 1903* (London, 1904), p. 185.

[26] Bok, *Keys to Success,* p. 100.

[27] Albert W. Atwood, *The Mind of the Millionaire* (New York, 1926), pp. 6–7.

[28] Quoted in Owen, *Success in Life,* p. 160.

[29] John D. Rockefeller, "Opportunity in America," *Cosmopolitan,* XLIII (1907), p. 369.

[30] Greeley, *Success in Business,* p. 14. On the virtue of frugality see also Emerson, *Works,* VI, 117; Wise, *Young Man's Counsellor,* pp. 129–140; Asher L. Smith and J. W. Hawxhurst, *How to Get Rich* (New York, 1866), p. 18; Mathews, *Getting On,* p. 295; Marden, *Entering Business,* p. 328.

[31] Carnegie, *Empire of Business,* pp. 95–96.

[32] Wesley Smead, *A Guide to Wealth* (Cincinnati, 1856), p. 80. For a discussion of the relation of reputation to credit consult F. M. Feiker, "The Profession of Commerce in the Making," *Annals of the American Academy of Political and Social Science,* CI (1922), 203–207.

[33] *Problem of Success,* p. 71.

[34] Wise, *Young Man's Counsellor,* p. 111.

[35] *Money for the Million,* p. 39.

[36] Bok, "Young Man in Business," *Cosmopolitan,* XVI (1894), 337; Bok, *Keys to Success,* p. 111.

[37] Mann, *Thoughts for a Young Man,* p. 72.

[38] Henry Livingston, ed., *The Money-Maker* (New York, 1868), p. 35.

[39] Ida C. Murray, "Small Things That Won My Success," *Ladies' Home Journal,* XXIV (1907), 66.

[40] William Holmes McGuffey, *The New McGuffey Third Reader* (Cincinnati, 1901), p. 59. See also Fergurson, *Young Man,* p. 38; Barnum, *Money-Getting,* p. 43; Eggleston, *How to Make a Living,* p. 36; Elbert H. Gary, "The Science of Business," in Harriet Blackstone, ed., *The Best American Orations of Today* (New York, 1926), pp. 335–336.

[41] Owen, *Success in Life,* p. 56.

[42] Edward Gray, "Some of the Essentials to Business Success," *Chautauquan,* XV (1892), 302.

[43] Edward Bok, "The Employer and the Young Man," *Cosmopolitan,* XVI (1894), 731.

[44] Rockefeller, "Opportunity in America," *Cosmopolitan,* XLIII (1907), 369.

[45] Barnum, *Money-Getting,* p. 31.

[46] Bok, *Keys to Success,* p. 103. See also Walter T. Field, *What is Success?* (Boston, 1910), p. 19.

[47] Gray, "Essentials to Business Success," *Chautauquan,* XV (1892), 302–303.

[48] Marden, *Entering Business,* p. 83.

[49] Charles R. Van Hise, *The Attainment of Success* (Madison, 1907), p. 9. See also Herbert J. Hapgood, "Kind of Men Employers Want," *World's Work,* XI (1906), 7463.

[50] Schwab, *Succeeding,* p. 10.

[51] Marden, *Entering Business,* p. 100.

CHAPTER IV.

[1] The basic book on this subject is Max Weber, *The Protestant Ethic and the Spirit of Capitalism* (New York, 1930). Weber's thesis is that the Protestant Reformation prepared the way for the development of the capitalist spirit. This thesis is also defended in William Cunningham, *Christianity and Economic Science* (London, 1914), and in Ernst Troeltsch, *Protestantism and Progress* (New York, 1912), and *The Social Teaching of the Christian Churches* (2 vols., New York, 1931). Richard Tawney, *Religion and the Rise of Capitalism* (New York, 1926) reverses Weber's emphasis by contending that the Protestant ethic was a by-product of modern capitalism. For further consideration of this matter, see Kemper Fullerton, "Calvinism and Capitalism," *Harvard Theological Review,* XXI (1928), 163–195, and Frank H. Knight, "Historical and Theoretical Issues in the Problem of Modern Capitalism," *Journal of Economic History,* I (1928), 119–136.

[2] Weber, *Protestant Ethic,* p. 180.

[3] Tawney, *Religion and the Rise of Capitalism,* pp. 163, 199.

[4] For data on the religious affiliations of business leaders, see Miller, "American Historians and the Business Elite," *Journal of Economic History,* IX (1949), 203.

[5] *Ibid.,* 200, 202. Of the 187 businessmen included in this survey, a majority came from families that had been in America for several generations. Three-fourths of these families originated in the British Isles.

[6] Perhaps the Lutheran failure to glorify the pursuit of wealth can be explained in terms of Luther's conception of the calling. Luther believed that agricultural callings were most honorable, and looked with disfavor on the activities of the banking and trading classes. He also believed that man should remain in the social position into which he had been born. In the Lutheran conception it was against all moral law to wish to rise in the world, or improve one's manner of living. Troeltsch, *Social Teaching,* II, 555, 814; Weber, *Protestant Ethic,* pp. 82–85; Tawney, *Religion and the Rise of Capitalism,* pp. 79–80.

[7] For self-help sermons by Episcopal clergymen, see Harry Croswell, "A Few Thoughts for Young Men," in James J.

Brenton, ed., *Voices from the Press* (New York, 1850), pp. 121–134; Gregory T. Bedell, *Labor and Profits: New Year Thoughts* (New York, 1858); Thomas P. Tyler, *The Elements Essential to Success in Life* (Hartford, Conn., 1856).

[8] Russel Crouse, ed., *Struggling Upward and Other Works* (New York, 1945), pp. viii–ix. For Alger's life see Herbert R. Mayes, *Alger; a Biography Without a Hero* (New York, 1928).

[9] "How to Make a Fortune," *Ladies' Repository,* XVIII (1858), 134.

[10] Matthew H. Smith, "The Elements of Business Success," *Hunt's Merchants' Magazine,* XXXI (1854), 56.

[11] Quoted in Hunt, *Worth and Wealth,* pp. 253–254. On the spiritual aspects of business, see also Andrew A. Lipscomb, "Success in Life," *Harper's New Monthly Magazine,* XIV (1857), 266–270.

[12] Masden, *Sacredness of Business,* p. 6.

[13] Lyman Abbott, "Righteousness," *Outlook,* XCIV (1910), 576. See also Lipscomb, "Success in Life," *Harper's,* XIV (1857), 267.

[14] Wise, *Young Man's Counsellor,* p. 127. See also Beecher, *Seven Lectures,* p. 11; Bedell, *Labor and Profits,* p. 6; Smith, "Elements of Business Success," *Hunt's Merchants' Magazine,* XXXI (1854), 56–57.

[15] Carnegie, *Empire of Business,* p. 128.

[16] Wise, *Young Man's Counsellor,* pp. 129–130.

[17] Marden, *Entering Business,* p. 328.

[18] Henry Ward Beecher, *Common Sense for Young Men on the Subject of Temperance* (New York, 1871), pp. 11–12.

[19] Bedell, *Labor and Profits,* p. 6.

[20] John W. Chadwick, *Rich and Poor* (Boston, 1885), p. 89.

[21] Russell H. Conwell, *Acres of Diamonds* (New York, 1915), p. 19.

[22] William Lawrence, "Relation of Wealth to Morals," *World's Work,* I (1901), 287. See also William S. Speer, *The Law of Success* (Nashville, 1885), pp. 188–189.

[23] Timothy S. Arthur, "Rich and Poor," in Anna Wilmot, ed., *The American Keepsake* (New York, 1851), p. 20.

[24] Van Doren, *Mercantile Morals,* p. 125.

[25] *Money for the Million,* p. 58.

[26] Speer, *Law of Success,* p. 241. In 1912 a compiler of a self-help handbook asked more than 300 successful men what book they would recommend to the ambitious young man. To nobody's surprise his correspondents named the Bible more often than any other book. Nathaniel C. Fowler, *The Boy: How to Help Him Succeed* (New York, 1912), p. 158.

[27] Bok, *Keys to Success,* pp. 116–117.

[28] For the religious activities of post–Civil-War business leaders, consult Matthew H. Smith, *Twenty Years Among the Bulls and Bears of Wall Street* (Hartford, Conn., 1870), pp. 414–421, and Matthew Josephson, *The Robber Barons* (New York, 1934), pp. 317–323.

[29] Bouck White, *The Book of Daniel Drew* (New York, 1937), p. 128.

[30] Smith, *Bulls and Bears of Wall Street,* pp. 332–333; Scoville, *Old Merchants,* I, 155.

[31] Scoville, *Old Merchants,* I, 230. Tappan also forbade his clerks to drink, visit houses of ill fame, indulge in "fast habits," attend the theater, associate with members of the theatrical profession, or stay out after 10 P.M.

[32] Gray, "Essentials to Business Success," *Chautauquan,* XV (1892), 303.

[33] Van Doren, *Mercantile Morals,* p. 265.

[34] Reade, *Money,* p. 100.

[35] Crafts, *Successful Men,* pp. 14–15. Crafts claimed that in sending questionnaires to businessmen he shunned those who had dubious reputations.

[36] Smith, *Successful Folks,* p. 13.

[37] Augusta Moore, ed., *Notes from Plymouth Pulpit* (New York, 1859), pp. 250–251.

[38] Conwell, *Acres of Diamonds,* pp. 34–35. See also Lyman Abbott, ed., *How to Succeed* (New York, 1882), p. 126; Channing, *Works,* p. 25.

[39] White, *Daniel Drew,* p. 308.

[40] Beecher, *Seven Lectures,* pp. 36–37, 56, 76.

[41] Van Doren, *Mercantile Morals,* p. 267.

[42] Beecher, *Seven Lectures,* p. 76.

[43] Van Doren, *Mercantile Morals,* p. 33.

[44] Moore, ed., *Plymouth Pulpit,* p. 53. See also Abbott, "Righteousness," *Outlook,* XCIV (1910), 578.

[45] Conwell, *Acres of Diamonds,* p. 24.

[46] Emerson, *Works,* VI, 97.

[47] Carnegie, *Gospel of Wealth,* pp. 74–76.

CHAPTER V.

[1] Arthur, *Advice to Young Men,* pp. 158–159.

[2] Hunt, *Worth and Wealth,* p. 150. See also Mann, *Thoughts for a Young Man,* pp. 72–73; Wise, *Young Man's Counsellor,* p. 107; David H. Agnew, "Conditions for Honorable Success in Life-Work," *Penn Monthly,* XII (1881), 916, 927; Edward A. Filene, "A Simple Code of Business Ethics," *Annals of the American Academy of Political and Social Science,* CI (1922), 224–225.

[3] Carnegie, *Empire of Business,* pp. 208–209. When Carnegie eulogized Ezra Cornell at Cornell University in 1907 he made much of the fact that Cornell had made his fortune through hard work and careful investments, "speculation having no place in it." Carnegie, *Ezra Cornell* (New York, 1907), pp. 11–12. Herbert N. Casson praised Carnegie on similar grounds, saying that his fortune "was not gained by a throw of the Wall Street dice or a speculation which scattered the seeds of future bankruptcies." Casson, "Rise of Andrew Carnegie," *Munsey's Magazine,* XXXV (1906), 327.

[4] Carnegie, *Empire of Business,* p. 8.

[5] Arthur, *Advice to Young Men,* pp. 161–162.

[6] Hunt, *Worth and Wealth,* pp. 72–73.

[7] Rockefeller, "Opportunity," *Cosmopolitan,* XLIII (1907), 369.

[8] Carnegie, *Empire of Business,* p. 8.

[9] *Problem of Success,* p. 155.

[10] *Money for the Million,* p. 28.

[11] Mann, *Thoughts for a Young Man,* p. 64.

[12] Maher, *Road to Riches,* p. 8. See also Mills, *Money Making,* pp. 170, 172–173; Frost, *Young Merchant,* p. 69; Simms, *Secrets of Success,* p. 14; Smead, *Guide to Wealth,* pp. 58–62.

[13] Marden, *Entering Business,* p. 244.

[14] *Ibid.*, p. 250. See also Edwin T. Freedley, *The Secret of Success in Life* (Philadelphia, 1881), p. 227; Maher, *Road to Riches,* pp. 156–158; Reade, *Money,* pp. 76–77.

[15] Mills, *Money Making,* p. 208.

[16] Beecher, *Seven Lectures,* p. 75.

[17] *How to Become Rich* (New York, 1878), pp. 5–6.

[18] Carnegie, *Gospel of Wealth,* p. 64.

[19] Quoted in William J. Ghent, *Our Benevolent Feudalism* (New York, 1902), p. 29.

[20] *Problem of Success,* p. 251; A. E. Swoyer, "Push or Pull?" *Overland Monthly,* LIX (1912), 548–549.

[21] Berton Braley, "Business is Business," *Nation's Business,* V (1917), 34–35.

[22] Richard Hofstadter, *Social Darwinism in American Thought, 1860–1915* (Philadelphia, 1945), pp. 30–32.

[23] *Money for the Million,* p. 15.

[24] Grover Cleveland, *The Self-Made Man in American Life* (New York, 1897), p. 24.

[25] Carnegie, "How Men Get Rich, and the Right View of Wealth," *World's Work,* XVII (1908), 11052.

[26] Quoted in Thomas A. Bland, *How to Grow Rich* (Washington, 1881), p. 18.

[27] Rockefeller, "Opportunity in America," *Cosmopolitan,* XLIII (1907), 369.

[28] Conwell, *Acres of Diamonds,* p. 30. For additional criticism of inheritances, see Mann, *Thoughts for a Young Man,* pp. 45–46; Crafts, *Successful Men,* p. 24; Cushman, *Elements of Success,* p. 9; Smead, *Guide to Wealth,* pp. 102–103; James D. Adams, "The Son of the Old Man and His Chances of Business Success," *Current Opinion,* LVII (1914), 358–361.

[29] Carnegie, *Gospel of Wealth,* p. 55.

[30] Carnegie, "How Men Get Rich," *World's Work,* XVII (1908), 11050.

[31] Craig, ed., *Room at the Top,* p. 46.

[32] Smith, *Bulls and Bears of Wall Street,* pp. 90, 175.

[33] Sorokin, "American Millionaires," *Journal of Social Forces,* III (1925), 635; Mills, "Business Elite," *Tasks of Economic History,* Supplement V (1945), pp. 29, 32; Taussig and Joslyn, *Business Leaders,* p. 116.

[34] Carnegie, *Gospel of Wealth,* p. 70.

[35] Carnegie, *Empire of Business,* p. 143.

CHAPTER VI.

[1] Carnegie, *Triumphant Democracy* (New York, 1893), p. 101.

[2] Sorokin, "American Millionaires," *Journal of Social Forces,* III (1925), 637; Edwin G. Dexter, "A Study of 20th Century Success," *Popular Science Monthly,* LXI (1902), 248.

[3] An unidentified industrialist, quoted in Charles F. Thwing, *College Training and the Business Man* (New York, 1904), p. 5.

[4] Carnegie, *Empire of Business,* p. 197.

[5] Owen, *Success in Life,* p. 55.

[6] Mills, *Money Making,* pp. 131–132. See also Julia E. McConaughy, *Capital for Working Boys* (Boston, 1883), p. 66; Reade, *Money,* p. 533. Before his conversion to Socialism even Eugene V. Debs urged the men of his railway union to read and study, with a view to winning promotions to positions of influence in the railroad industry. Debs, "Time is Money," *Locomotive Firemen's Magazine,* XIII (1889), 202–203.

[7] Mills, *Money Making,* p. 135.

[8] White, *Daniel Drew,* p. 9.

[9] Nathaniel Hawthorne, *The Complete Writings of Nathaniel Hawthorne* (22 vols., Boston, 1900), XX, 102–103.

[10] Sidney Ditzion, "Mechanics and Mercantile Libraries," *The Library Quarterly,* X (1940), 199–200.

[11] For rule-of-thumb estimates of the educational status of the business elite, see Beach, *Wealth and Pedigree* (4th edition), p. 7; Bok, "Young Man in Business," *Cosmopolitan,* XVI (1894), 338; Freedley, *Secret of Success,* p. 62; Carnegie, *Empire of Business,* pp. 106–113; Albion, *Rise of New York Port,* p. 252. For more reliable data, see Dexter, "20th Century Success," *Popular Science Monthly,* LXI (1902), 242, 248, 249; Sorokin, "American Millionaires," *Journal of Social Forces,* III (1925), 637; Mills, "Business Elite," *Tasks of Economic History,* Supplement V (1945), 35–36.

[12] Greeley, *Success in Business,* p. 12; Edwin T. Freedley, *A Practical Treatise on Business* (Philadelphia, 1854), p. 37;

Carnegie, *Empire of Business,* pp. 80, 110; Bok, "Young Man in Business," *Cosmopolitan,* XVI (1894), 338.

[13] Elbert Hubbard, *A Message to Garcia* (New York, 1926), p. 5. See also Mosely, *Reports of the Mosely Educational Commission,* p. 396; Wells, *How to Do Business,* pp. 29–30; Freedley, *Practical Treatise on Business,* p. 37, and *Secret of Success,* p. 62.

[14] White, *Daniel Drew,* pp. 309–310.

[15] McCurdy, *Win Who Will,* p. 17. See also Speer, *Law of Success,* pp. 252–255; Greeley, *Success in Business,* p. 12.

[16] Carnegie, *Empire of Business,* pp. 80–81.

[17] Garfield, *Elements of Success,* p. 2.

[18] O'Connor, *Mellon's Millions,* p. 21; Freedley, *Practical Treatise on Business,* p. 37; Mosely, *Reports of the Mosely Educational Commission,* p. 396.

[19] Carnegie, *Empire of Business,* p. 110.

[20] Quoted in Thwing, *College Training,* p. 20.

[21] Quoted in Charles F. Thwing, "College Training and the Business Man," *North American Review,* CLXXVII (1903), 599. See also Thwing, *College Training,* pp. 4–6; Heermans, *Nuggets of Gold,* pp. 41–49; Maher, *Road to Riches,* pp. 13–14.

[22] Quoted in Thwing, *College Training,* p. 27.

[23] William A. Croffut, *The Vanderbilts and the Story of Their Fortune* (New York, 1886), p. 137.

[24] Carnegie, *Empire of Business,* p. 113.

[25] Charles W. Eliot, "Uses of Education for Business," in Blackstone, ed., *Best American Orations,* p. 168.

[26] Mosely, *Reports of the Mosely Educational Commission,* pp. 187, 337–338.

[27] *Problem of Success,* p. 170.

[28] Masden, *Sacredness of Business,* p. 9; Cleveland, *Self-Made Man,* p. 15.

[29] James B. Dill, "The College Man and the Corporate Proposition," *Munsey's Magazine,* XXIV (1900), p. 148. See also Henry H. Lewis, "Are Young Men's Chances Less?" *World's Work,* I (1900), 173; Robert H. Thurston, "College-Man as Leader in the World's Work," *Popular Science Monthly,* LX (1902), 358; Mosely, *Reports of the Mosely Educational Commission,* pp. 56–57.

[30] Miller, "American Historians and the Business Elite," *Journal of Economic History,* IX (1949), pp. 207–208; Taussig and Joslyn, *American Business Leaders,* p. 162.

[31] Thurston, "College Man," *Popular Science Monthly,* LX (1902), 353; Mosely, *Reports of the Mosely Educational Commission,* pp. 60, 187, 337.

[32] Quoted in Thwing, *College Training,* p. 28; Marden, *Entering Business,* p. 19.

[33] Garfield, *Elements of Success,* pp. 1–2.

[34] Quoted in Mosely, *Reports of the Mosely Educational Commission,* p. 187.

[35] Rockefeller, "Opportunity," *Cosmopolitan,* XLIII (1907), 368, 370.

[36] Carnegie, *Empire of Business,* pp. 81, 111.

[37] "Brains and Education as Capital," *Commercial and Financial Chronicle,* CII (1916), 1845.

[38] Gary, "Science of Business," in Blackstone, ed., *Best American Orations,* p. 334.

[39] J. Jastrow, "Higher Education for Business Men in the United States and Germany," in United States Bureau of Education, *Report of the Commissioner of Education, 1905* (Washington, 1907), I, 109–110.

[40] *Ibid.,* I, 98.

[41] Schwab, *Succeeding,* pp. 30, 34.

CHAPTER VII.

[1] Bell, "Worship of Success," in Northup, ed., *Phi Beta Kappa Orations,* p. 176.

[2] Wright, "Franklin's Legacy," *Virginia Quarterly Review,* XXII (1946), 268. By way of verifying Wright's impressions the author checked the publication dates of 105 nineteenth-century success manuals, held by the Library of Congress. Of this number 16 were published before the Civil War, and 89 after.

[3] The author checked the place of publication of 102 self-help handbooks, and discovered that 90 were published in New England, the Middle Atlantic states, and the Middle West, and only 12 in other sections of the country. Almost half of the total originated in New York.

Alfred Whitney Griswold's study of the success cult, New Thought, showed that as of 1890 its adherents lived principally in Boston, New York, Chicago, Kansas City, and San Francisco. New Thought had no vogue in the South or other predominantly rural sections. See Alfred W. Griswold, "New Thought: a Cult of Success," *The American Journal of Sociology,* XL (1934), 309–318.

[4] Frank L. Mott, *Golden Multitudes* (New York, 1947), p. 97.

[5] Washington Irving, *Astoria* (New York, 1849), p. 52.

[6] Bell, "Worship of Success," in Northup, ed., *Phi Beta Kappa Orations,* p. 176.

[7] These questions appear in Crafts, *Successful Men,* pp. 13–14, and Nathaniel C. Fowler, *The Boy: How to Help Him Succeed* (New York, 1912), pp. 130–152. Edwin T. Freedley was one of the first to solicit opinions from millionaires on how to make money. See Freedley, *Practical Treatise on Business,* pp. 176–191, 298–304. See also Francis E. Clark, *Our Business Boys* (Boston, 1884), and *Danger Signals, the Enemies of Youth from the Business Man's Standpoint* (Boston, 1885), two volumes based on information provided by the businessmen of Portland, Maine. Speer, *Law of Success,* summarizes the results of 1200 interviews with prominent men of the South and Southwest. Speer was especially interested in the mottoes which helped men to success.

[8] Mathews, *Getting On,* p. vi.

[9] T. D. MacGregor, "Mobilizing American Dollars," *Bankers Magazine,* XCI (1915), 658.

[10] Livingston, ed., *Money-Maker,* p. 6.

[11] Greeley, *Success in Business,* p. 2.

[12] Speer, *Law of Success,* pp. 250–251.

[13] Marden, *Entering Business,* pp. 139–140.

[14] William M. Thayer, "Teachers' Aid to Self-Help," *Education,* XII (1892), 597.

[15] Mann, *Thoughts for a Young Man,* pp. 52–60.

[16] Benjamin Franklin, *Extracts from the Autobiography and Other Writings of Benjamin Franklin* (Boston, 1906).

[17] For an analysis of the success theme in the McGuffey readers, see Richard D. Mosier, *Making the American Mind* (New York, 1947), pp. 99–123.

[18] Mathews, *Getting On,* p. v.

[19] *Money for the Million,* pp. 47; McCurdy, *Win Who Will,* p. 27.

[20] *The Dial,* XX (1896), 143.

[21] Charles C. B. Seymour, *Self-Made Men* (New York, 1858), Preface.

[22] Craig, ed., *Room at the Top,* p. 155.

[23] *Men Who Have Risen* (New York, 1859), pp. 110, 118–120.

[24] Livingston, ed., *Money-Maker,* p. 11.

[25] Smith, *Bulls and Bears of Wall Street,* p. 195.

[26] McCurdy, *Win Who Will,* p. 6. For other statements of this objective, see Mills, *Money Making,* p. 26; Frost, *Young Merchant,* pp. 10–11; Smead, *Guide to Wealth,* pp. 67–68.

[27] Freedley, *Secret of Success,* p. 1; Speer, *Law of Success,* p. 17.

CHAPTER VIII.

[1] Paul L. Ford, ed., *The Writings of Thomas Jefferson* (10 vols., New York, 1892–99), IV, 143, X, 107; Thomas Jefferson, *Notes on Virginia* (Richmond, 1853), p. 176.

[2] James Fenimore Cooper, *The American Democrat* (Cooperstown, N. Y., 1838), pp. 140, 168–169.

[3] Bradford Torrey, ed., *The Writings of Henry David Thoreau* (20 vols., Boston, 1906), II, 77, XII, 106.

[4] John H. Ingram, ed., *The Works of Edgar Allan Poe* (4 vols., London, 1899), II, 479.

[5] "Mammon," *The Cabinet of Instruction, Literature and Amusement,* I (1829), 300.

[6] Rebecca Harding Davis, "The Disease of Money-Getting," *Independent,* LIV (1902), 1458.

[7] Bernard DeVoto, ed., *Mark Twain in Eruption* (New York, 1940), p. 77.

[8] Bell, "Worship of Success," in Northup, ed., *Phi Beta Kappa Orations,* p. 186.

[9] Torrey, ed., *Writings of Thoreau,* IV, 456–457.

[10] "The Sacrifice of the Present," *Current Literature,* XXVII (1900), 118.

[11] Davis, "Disease of Money-Getting," *Independent,* LIV (1902), 1459.

[12] Francis Bellamy, "Successful Men Who Are Not Rich," *Everybody's Magazine,* IX (1903), 607–608.

[13] Edgar Allan Poe, "The Business Man," in *Complete Tales and Poems of Edgar Allan Poe* (New York, 1938), p. 413.

[14] Holmes, *Autocrat of the Breakfast Table,* pp. 19–23.

[15] George Lathrop, ed., *The Complete Works of Nathaniel Hawthorne* (12 vols., Boston, 1886), XII, 202.

[16] James Russell Lowell, *The Writings of James Russell Lowell in Prose and Poetry* (7 vols., Boston, 1899), II, 250, 292–293.

[17] G. M. Kellogg, "Self-Made Men," *Lakeside Monthly,* II (1869), 37–38. See also University of Wisconsin, *The University Press,* September 15, 1871, for an answer to Horace Greeley's assaults on the higher learning.

[18] Sheldon, "College-Bred Men," *New Englander,* LVI (1892), 189–209.

[19] Theodore Roosevelt, *The Strenuous Life* (New York, 1903), pp. 115–116.

[20] Quoted in Josephson, *Robber Barons,* p. 337. See also Charles Whibley, "The American Millionaire," *Bookman,* XXV (1907), 577–583. Whibley criticized American self-made men from the vantage point of the English aristocracy.

[21] Coan, "Successful People," *Galaxy,* XI (1871), 219–228.

[22] Quoted in Edward Atkinson, *Industrial Exhibitions: Their True Function in Connection with Industrial Education* (Boston, 1882), p. 22.

[23] Lester F. Ward, "Broadening the Way to Success," *The Forum,* II (1886), 340–350.

[24] Carnegie, *Empire of Business,* p. 14.

[25] Marden, *Entering Business,* p. 110.

[26] *Ibid.,* p. 369.

[27] *Problem of Success,* p. 189. See also Conwell, *Acres of Diamonds,* p. 53; "What is Success?" *Current Literature,* XXXV (1903), 355; Thurston, "College Man," *Popular Science Monthly,* LX (1902), 350.

[28] Marden, *Entering Business,* pp. 9, 110.

[29] "About Opportunities," *World's Work,* XI (1906), 7035.

[30] William James Ghent, *Socialism and Success* (New York, 1910), pp. 18–19, 24.

[31] "What is Success?", *Current Literature,* XXXV (1903), 355.

[32] Miller, "American Historians and the Business Elite," *Journal of Economic History,* IX (1949), 206; Mills, "Business Elite," *Tasks of Economic History,* Supplement V (1945), 30, 44; Sorokin, "American Millionaires," *Journal of Social Forces,* III (1925), 636.

[33] Henry George, *Progress and Poverty* (Modern Library edition, New York, n.d.), pp. 403–407.

[34] Bland, *How to Grow Rich,* pp. 3–15, 17.

[35] Henry D. Lloyd, *Lords of Industry* (New York, 1910), p. 46.

[36] Gustavus Myers, *The History of the Great American Fortunes* (3 vols., New York, 1910), I, iii.

[37] Brander Matthews, "Standards of Success," *Forum,* LXII (1909), 309.

[38] Joseph D. Miller, "Apostles of Autolatry," *Arena,* XXIV (1900), 610.

[39] "What is Success?" *Current Literature,* XXXV (1903), 355.

[40] H. Lamont, "The Young Man and the World," *Nation,* LXXXI (1905), 376–377.

[41] "A Passing Humbug," *The Bookman,* XXXVI (1912), 18.

CHAPTER IX.

[1] Quoted in Hunt, *Worth and Wealth,* p. 351.

[2] Emerson, *Works,* VI, 92.

[3] Carl Van Doren, ed., *Benjamin Franklin's Autobiographical Writings* (New York, 1945), pp. 264–265.

[4] Emerson, *Works,* VI, 91–92.

[5] Quoted in Casson, "Rise of Andrew Carnegie," *Munsey's Magazine,* XXV (1906), 321.

[6] *Hunt's Merchants' Magazine,* I (1839), 2.

[7] Richard Hofstadter, *The American Political Tradition and the Men Who Made It* (New York, 1948), pp. 102–106.

[8] Seth Ames, ed., *Works of Fisher Ames* (2 vols., Boston, 1854), II, 211.

[9] Samuel Harden Church, *Ostentatious Wealth and Class Feel-*

ing (n.p., 1907), p. 11. See also Charles Kendall Adams, *The Limitations of Reform* (Madison, 1894), p. 5; Lawrence, "Relation of Wealth to Morals," *World's Work,* I (1901), 288.

[10] Smead, *Guide to Wealth,* p. 8. See also Margaret B. Wilson, ed., *A Carnegie Anthology* (New York, 1915), p. 150; Livingston, ed., *Money-Maker,* p. 11; Fergurson, *Young Man,* pp. 30–31, 34–35; Wise, *Young Man's Counsellor,* p. 91; Garfield, *Elements of Success,* p. 4.

[11] Beecher, *Seven Lectures,* p. 15.

[12] "Success as Mere Luck," *Literary Digest,* CI (1929), 9. See also Owen, *Success in Life,* pp. 245, 259; Crafts, *Successful Men,* pp. 15–16.

[13] Carnegie, *Empire of Business,* p. 15.

[14] Mathews, *Getting On,* p. 295.

[15] Speer, *Law of Success,* p. 178.

[16] Adams, *Limitations of Reform,* pp. 16–17.

[17] Lyman Abbott, "Willing to Work," *Outlook,* LXXXIX (1908), 643.

[18] Greeley, *Success in Business,* pp. 5–6, 16.

[19] Heermans, *Nuggets of Gold,* pp. 169–170. See also *Money for the Million,* p. 47; McCurdy, *Win Who Will,* p. 27.

[20] *Problem of Success,* p. viii.

[21] Abbott, "Willing to Work," *Outlook,* LXXXIX (1908), 643.

[22] For Everett's remarks, see Frost, *Young Merchant,* p. 132.

[23] Channing, "The Present Age," *Works,* p. 168.

[24] Smith, "Elements of Business Success," *Hunt's Merchants' Magazine,* XXXI (1854), 61–62.

[25] Andrew Carnegie, *James Watt* (New York, 1905), p. 33.

[26] Cleveland, *Self-Made Man,* pp. 16–17, 29, 32.

[27] James M. Beck, *The Youthful Franklin* (Philadelphia, 1914), pp. 9–10.

[28] Carnegie, *Gospel of Wealth,* pp. xi–xii.

[29] Hubbard, *Message to Garcia,* pp. 7–8.

[30] Carnegie, *Gospel of Wealth,* pp. 48, 52–53.

[31] Lawrence, "Relation of Wealth to Morals," *World's Work,* I (1901), 288–289.

[32] Thurston, "College Man," *Popular Science Monthly,* LX (1902), 349. See also C. M. Keys, "How Men Get Rich Now," *World's Work,* XI (1906), 7066–7071; Abbott, "Righteousness,"

Outlook, XCIV (1910), 577; Carnegie, *Empire of Business,* pp. 132, 137.

[33] Quoted in Lewis, "Are Young Men's Chances Less?" *World's Work,* I (1900), 172. For Russell Sage's views, see *Problem of Success,* p. 69. See also Leroy Scott, "Need Any Man Lack a Job?" *World's Work,* X (1905), 6660.

[34] Bok, "Young Man in Business," *Cosmopolitan,* XVI (1894), 333.

[35] Marden, *Entering Business,* p. 120. See also Herbert J. Hapgood, "The Search for Men," *Harper's Monthly Magazine,* CXI (1905), 267.

[36] Quoted in Lewis, "Are Young Men's Chances Less?" *World's Work,* I (1900), 171.

[37] Gary, "Science of Business," in Blackstone, ed., *Best American Orations,* p. 338. See also Church, *Ostentatious Wealth,* p. 11.

[38] *Problem of Success,* p. 246; Schwab, *Succeeding,* p. 26.

[39] Rockefeller, "Opportunity in America," *Cosmopolitan,* XLIII (1907), 368–372.

[40] John D. Rockefeller, Jr., *Character the Foundation of Successful Business* (n.p., n.d.), p. 14. Rockefeller delivered this address to the Twenty-Six Broadway Club, December 1, 1927.

[41] "Helping to Success," *The Commercial and Financial Chronicle,* CII (1916), 926.

EPILOGUE

[1] Richard J. Walsh, "The Doom of the Self-Made Man," *Century Magazine,* CIX (December, 1924), 258.

[2] Bruce Barton, "Their Strength Was to Sit Still," *American Magazine,* CVIII (October, 1929), 78.

[3] Lawrence W. Rogers, *Success; Fact or Fiction?* (New York, 1930), p. 4.

[4] Roger W. Babson, "What the Depression is Teaching," *Review of Reviews,* LXXXV (May, 1932), 22.

[5] Quoted in Albert Shaw, "Roger Babson Reflects," *Review of Reviews,* LXXXV (May, 1932), 25.

[6] Robert S. and Helen M. Lynd, *Middletown in Transition* (New York, 1937), pp. 242, 406–407, 420.

[7] Hadley Cantril, ed., *Public Opinion, 1935–1946* (Princeton,

New Jersey, 1951), pp. 829–831. This volume summarizes the results of eighteen polls on the subject of success.

A NOTE ON SOURCES

Chapter VII, Preach the Gospel, is in itself an extended analysis of success literature, and the notes throughout indicate source material. In lieu of the usual listing of a complete bibliography, the following paragraphs discuss the general body of available literature and offer some indication of the purposes which a few of the more important items may serve in the interpretation of the self-help theme in America.

There is considerable secondary material relating to various aspects of the rags-to-riches idea, but no complete study which treats the idea in its historical contexts. The best brief survey is in Merle E. Curti, *The Growth of American Thought* (New York, 1943). Louis B. Wright, *Middle-Class Culture in Elizabethan England* (Chapel Hill, 1935) discusses seventeenth-century English self-help ideas, and their transmission to America. A more complete treatment of colonial economic ideas is available in E. A. J. Johnson, *American Economic Thought in the 17th Century* (London, 1932). There is also a mine of essential background information in Joseph Dorfman, *The Economic Mind in American Civilization* (3 vols., New York, 1946–). A study which impinges more directly on the self-help idea is Donald W. McConnell, *Economic Virtues in the United States* (New York, 1930), which shows how competing economic interest groups interpreted the basic virtues in different ways. Despite its alluring title, Albert W. Atwood, *The Mind of the Millionaire* (New York, 1926) offers little more than the assurance that millionaires are human and men of mixed motives. It is an apology, not a critical study. Miriam Beard, *A History of the Business Man* (New York, 1938), is a more substantial treatment, but it deals primarily with European economic developments.

Sociologists, economists and business historians have provided a broad background of precise information about the social origins and characteristics of business leaders, and the means by which they have risen. Their findings sometimes support, but more often contradict the explanations offered in the rags-to-riches literature. Pitirim Sorokin, *Social Mobility* (New York, 1927), was a pioneer study of the ways and means by which individuals changed status in society. Sorokin also broke new ground in his statistical analysis of "American Millionaires and Multi-Millionaires," *Journal of Social Forces,* III (1925), 627–640. Another instructive statistical study is C. Wright Mills, "The American Business Elite: a Collective Portrait," *Journal of Economic History,* Supplement V (1945), 20–44, which covers the careers of outstanding businessmen listed in the *Dictionary of American Biography*. William Miller, "American Historians and the Business Elite," *Journal of Economic History,* IX (1949), 184–208, shows that few of the nation's top executives in the first decade of the twentieth century were self-made men. Two economists, Frank W. Taussig and C. S. Joslyn, used the questionnaire method to get data for *American Business Leaders* (New York, 1932), a study which overemphasizes personal factors in success.

The question of whether country boys won more successes than city boys has been hotly debated. The most recent statistical surveys take some of the honor away from country boys, but Robert G. Albion, *The Rise of New York Port* (New York, 1939), argues that they took most of the honors in pre–Civil-War New York. For other views on this and related issues, see W. J. Spillman, "The Country Boy," *Science,* XXX (1909), 405–407; Frederick A. Woods, "City Boys versus Country Boys," *Science,* XXIX (1909), 577–579; Henry Cabot Lodge, "Distribution of Ability in the United States," *Century Magazine,* XLII (1891), 687–694; Edwin G. Dexter, "A Study of Twentieth Century Success," *Popular Science Monthly,* LXI (1902), 241–251; Dumas Malone, "The Geography of American Achievement," *Atlantic Monthly,* CLIV (1934), 669–679; and Stephen S. Visher, *Geography of American Notables* (Bloomington, Ind., 1928).

Biographies of business leaders contributed to the orientation of this study. A few of the most useful accounts where Burton J. Hendrick, *The Life of Andrew Carnegie* (2 vols., Garden City, N. Y., 1932); Harvey O'Connor, *Mellon's Millions* (New York, 1933); Harry E. Wildes, *Lonely Midas; the Story of Stephen Girard* (New York, 1943); William A. Croffut, *The Vanderbilts and the Story of Their Fortune* (New York, 1886); Allan Nevins, *John D. Rockefeller* (2 vols., New York, 1940); John T. Flynn, *God's Gold* (New York, 1932); and Matthew Josephson, *The Robber Barons* (New York, 1934).

There are several excellent books on religion in relation to the idea of business success, but none tells the story in terms of America. The two basic studies are Max Weber, *The Protestant Ethic and the Spirit of Capitalism* (New York, 1930), and Richard H. Tawney, *Religion and the Rise of Capitalism* (New York, 1926). Other useful accounts are William Cunningham, *Christianity and Economic Science* (London, 1914), and two books by Ernst Troeltsch, *Protestantism and Progress* (New York, 1912), and *The Social Teaching of the Christian Churches* (2 vols., New York, 1931). The theoretical issues raised by these studies are explored in Kemper Fullerton, "Calvinism and Capitalism," *Harvard Theological Review,* XXI (1928), 163–195, and Frank H. Knight, "Historical and Theoretical Issues in the Problem of Modern Capitalism," *Journal of Economic History,* I (1928), 119–136. A. Whitney Griswold treats these matters in an American context in two noteworthy articles, "Three Puritans on Prosperity," *New England Quarterly,* VII (1934), 475–493, and "New Thought: a Cult of Success," *American Journal of Sociology,* XL (1934), 309–318.

Though this study owes much to secondary accounts, it owes more to primary materials, particularly the virginal literature of business success—the didactic guidebooks, addresses, essays and sermons which called young men to the quest for wealth. These items may be found in almost any library, but the richest collection is in the Library of Congress.

Manuscripts and newspapers did not contribute substantially to this study. The fundamentals of the success argument, having to do with industry, frugality, and sobriety, are invariably the same, regardless of the sources in which they appear. The advice which the wealthy businessman sends to his poor nephew by mail is the same as that which he offers at a commencement exercise, or in a newspaper interview, or in his book on how to make a million. The virtue which distinguishes one source from another in this field is not the virtue of reliability, but the virtue of accessibility. In respect to newspapers it is worth noting that some of the most popular success books appeared first in serial form in the papers. William Mathews, *Getting on in the World* (Chicago, 1874), was published originally in the Chicago *Tribune;* William H. Maher, *On the Road to Riches* (Toledo, 1876), made its debut in the Toledo *Blade;* and *The Problem of Success for Young Men and How to Solve It* (New York, 1903) appeared first in the Hearst newspapers.

Success novels, such as those of Horatio Alger, were also passed over, not because they are unimportant, but because they have already received more attention than the didactic guidebooks which offered direct advice on how to make money. Anyone interested in success fiction should consult Walter F. Taylor, *The Economic Novel in America* (Chapel Hill, 1942); Herbert R. Mayes, *Alger; a Biography Without a Hero* (New York, 1928); Russel Crouse, ed., *Struggling Upward and Other Works by Horatio Alger, Jr.* (New York, 1945); and E. Kenton, "Millions and Millionaires in Fiction," *Bookman,* XXXV (1912), 141–144, 319–322.

Benjamin Franklin was the most popular oracle of the American success cult, and its earliest hero. His sayings and essays on self-help can be found in John Bigelow, ed., *The Complete Writings of Benjamin Franklin* (10 vols., New York, 1887–88). For the best account of Franklin's life, see Carl Van Doren's biography, and his edition of *Benjamin Franklin's Autobiographical Writings* (New York, 1945). Louis B. Wright, "Franklin's Legacy to the Gilded Age," *Virginia Quarterly Review,* XXII (1946), 268–279, documents Franklin's influence on the success literature of the post–Civil-War period. For examples of the way conservative spokesmen used the Franklin legend, see two addresses, Robert C. Winthrop, *Oration at the Inauguration of the Statue of Benjamin Franklin* (Boston, 1856), and James M. Beck, *The Youthful Franklin* (Philadelphia, 1914).

Though success publishing reached its climax after the Civil War many important titles appeared earlier. In these early guides advice on financial affairs was often subordinate to advice on general moral deportment. Examples may be found in Frank Fergurson, *The Young Man* (Boston, 1848); Daniel Wise, *The Young Man's Counsellor* (New York, 1854); and Timothy S. Arthur, *Advice to Young Men on Their Duties and Conduct in*

Life (Boston, 1848). The same moral counsel appeared in books addressed more specifically to the prospective businessman, such as Louisa C. Tuthill, *The Merchant* (New York, 1850); and John Frost, *The Young Merchant* (Boston, 1841). Freeman Hunt was the leading pre–Civil-War authority on self-help. In addition to editing *Hunt's Merchants' Magazine,* a treasure trove of success material, he wrote *Worth and Wealth* (New York, 1856), and *Lives of American Merchants* (2 vols., New York, 1858). His closest rival was Edwin T. Freedley, author of *A Practical Treatise on Business* (Philadelphia, 1854), and *Leading Pursuits and Leading Men* (Philadelphia, 1856). New York and Philadelphia vied with one another in boasting of their wealthy men. This was implicit in Moses Y. Beach, *Wealth and Pedigree of the Wealthy Citizens of New York City* (New York, 1842), and *Wealth and Biography of the Wealthy Citizens of Philadelphia* (Philadelphia, 1845), published by a member of the Philadelphia bar.

Businessmen have always played an active part in publicizing the rags-to-riches idea. Sometimes they wrote success guides, such as Wesley Smead, *Guide to Wealth* (Cincinnati, 1856); James D. Mills, *The Art of Money Making* (New York, 1872); Phineas T. Barnum, *The Art of Money-Getting* (New York, 1882), *How I Made Millions* (Chicago, 1884), and *Dollars and Sense* (Chicago, 1890); Andrew Carnegie, *The Empire of Business* (New York, 1902); and Charles M. Schwab, *Succeeding with What You Have* (New York, 1917). Occasionally they delivered success orations. A few representative selections are Andrew Carnegie, *The Gospel of Wealth* (New York, 1892), *How I Served My Apprenticeship as a Business Man* (Boston, 1896), and *Ezra Cornell* (New York, 1907); Elbert H. Gary, "The Science of Business," in Harriet Blackstone, ed., *The Best American Orations of Today* (New York, 1926); and John D. Rockefeller, Jr., *Character the Foundation of Successful Business* (New York, 1927). Leading businessmen often answered questionnaires or granted interviews to writers who wished to offer authoritative advice. Books based on such material are William S. Speer, *The Law of Success* (Nashville, 1885); Wilbur F. Crafts, *Successful Men of Today and What They Say of Success* (New York, 1883); Francis E. Clark, *Our Business Boys*

(Boston, 1884); and Nathaniel C. Fowler, *The Boy: How to Help Him Succeed* (New York, 1912).

Biographies and autobiographies constitute an important source of material, because the rules of success were supposed to be implicit in the lives of men who had achieved it. The noteworthy autobiographies include P. T. Barnum, *Struggles and Triumphs* (Hartford, 1869); Henry Clews, *Twenty-Eight Years in Wall Street* (New York, 1887); Peter Cooper, *A Sketch of the Early Days and Business Life of Peter Cooper* (New York, 1877); Thomas Mellon, *Thomas Mellon and His Times* (Pittsburgh, 1885); Andrew Carnegie, *Autobiography of Andrew Carnegie* (Boston, 1920); and John D. Rockefeller, *Random Reminiscences of Men and Events* (New York, 1909). There is a wealth of rags-to-riches biography. William M. Thayer, *The Poor Boy and Merchant Prince* (New York, 1857) is the life of Amos Lawrence. John Wanamaker's story is told in Russell H. Conwell, *The Romantic Rise of a Great American* (New York, 1924). Elbert Hubbard, *Little Journeys to the Homes of Great Business Men* (2 vols., East Aurora, N. Y., 1909), sketches the lives of Stephen Girard, Philip Armour, John Jacob Astor, Peter Cooper, George Peabody, Alexander T. Stewart and others. Similar accounts may be found in James Parton, *Captains of Industry* (2 vols., Boston, 1884); Joseph A. Scoville, *The Old Merchants of New York City* (3 vols., New York, 1870); Matthew H. Smith, *Twenty Years Among the Bulls and Bears of Wall Street* (Hartford, 1870); and J. Chamberlain, *Makers of Millions* (Chicago, 1899).

Protestant clergymen were extremely active in the field of success publicity. Many of the general moral handbooks of the pre–Civil-War years were written by clergymen. Examples are John Todd, *The Young Man* (Northampton, Mass., 1845); Henry Ward Beecher, *Seven Lectures to Young Men* (Indianapolis, 1844); and William Van Doren, *Mercantile Morals* (New York, 1852). Of the later books, a few of the more important are Daniel Wise, *Uncrowned Kings* (New York, 1875); William Dale Owen, *Success in Life* (Chicago, 1878); Lyman Abbott, ed., *How to Succeed* (New York, 1882); and Francis E. Clark, *Our Business Boys* (Boston, 1884), and *Danger Signals, The Enemies of Youth, from the Business Man's Standpoint*

(Boston, 1885). The most significant essay by a clergyman is William Lawrence, "Relation of Wealth to Morals," *World's Work,* I (1901), 286–292. The classic success sermon is *Acres of Diamonds* (New York, 1915), which Russell Conwell delivered thousands of times. Other noteworthy sermons are Charles P. Masden, *The Sacredness of Business* (Milwaukee, 1898); John W. Chadwick, *Rich and Poor* (Boston, 1885); John Todd, *The Foundations of Success* (Northampton, Mass., 1843); and Thomas P. Tyler, *The Elements Essential to Success in Life* (Hartford, 1856).

Men of literary distinction rarely devoted whole books to the rags-to-riches theme, though they often commented upon it. The collected works of Emerson, Thoreau, Holmes, Hawthorne, Lowell and others have been used extensively in the preparation of this study. Books by men of lesser literary reputation are George Cary Eggleston, *How to Make a Living* (New York, 1875), and Edwin P. Whipple, *Success and Its Conditions* (Boston, 1877). Journalists have fat bibliographies in this field. A few of the more important titles are Timothy S. Arthur, *Rising in the World* (New York, 1848); Matthew H. Smith, *Successful Folks* (Hartford, 1878); Edward W. Bok, *Successward* (New York, 1899); William Mathews, *Getting on in the World* (Chicago, 1874); Edwin T. Freedley, *The Secret of Success in Life* (Philadelphia, 1881); Orison S. Marden, *Pushing to the Front* (Toledo, 1911), and *The Young Man Entering Business* (New York, 1903). The popular magazines have always featured self-help articles; these have been used extensively. Elbert Hubbard, *A Message to Garcia* (New York, 1926) is a classic among the short essays written by journalists. First published in 1899, it has been reprinted many times since. Orations by journalists include Matthew H. Smith, "The Elements of Business Success," *Hunt's Merchants' Magazine,* XXXI (1854), 56–62; Horace Greeley, *Success in Business* (New York, 1867), and *Practical Education* (New York, 1869); and Edward W. Bok, *The Keys to Success* (Philadelphia, 1898).

Phrenologists and vocational counselors wrote some of the most popular guides to wealth. Leading titles in this category are Samuel R. Wells, *How to Do Business* (New York, 1857); Nelson Sizer, *Choice of Pursuits* (New York, 1877), *The Royal*

Road to Wealth (New York, 1882), *The Road to Success* (New York, 1884); and Nathaniel C. Fowler, *The Boy: How to Help Him Succeed* (New York, 1912).

The role of the schools in inculcating success values is already well known. The best book on this subject is Merle E. Curti, *The Social Ideas of American Educators* (New York, 1935). Richard D. Mosier, *Making the American Mind* (New York, 1947) analyzes the social ideas of the McGuffey readers, but there is no substitute for the readers themselves. Another writer of school texts, William Makepeace Thayer, authored such books as *Onward to Fame and Fortune* (New York, 1897); *Success and Its Achievers* (Boston, 1891); and *Ethics of Success* (Boston, 1893). Educators often spoke on the subject of business success. Representatives orations are Horace Mann, *A Few Thoughts for a Young Man* (Boston, 1887); Charles R. Van Hise, *The Attainment of Success* (Madison, Wis., 1907); and Charles W. Eliot, "Uses of Education for Business," in Harriet Blackstone, ed., *The Best American Orations of Today* (New York, 1926). Two of the best sources on the attitudes of businessmen towards the higher learning are Charles F. Thwing, *College Training and the Business Man* (New York, 1904), and A. Mosely, *Reports of the Mosely Educational Commission to the United States of America, October–December, 1903* (London, 1904).

There is a substantial literature which criticizes the self-help idea and the values associated with it. Ham Jones, *About Money* (Boston, 1872), is a brief, satirical assault. *How to Grow Rich* (Washington, 1881), by Thomas A. Bland, a Southern antimonopolist, is equally short and equally critical. Lester F. Ward, "Broadening the Way to Success," *Forum,* II (1886), 340–350, is a carefully reasoned attack by a social scientist. Ward errs, however, in his contention that success apologists attribute success to inherited ability. Muckrakers and Socialists were effective critics of the self-help idea. Gustavus Myers, *History of the Great American Fortunes* (3 vols., New York, 1910), demonstrated that there were other factors besides virtue in the upbuilding of fortunes. For a strong criticism of the partnership of orthodox religion and business, see Bouck White, *The Book of Daniel Drew* (Garden City, N. Y., 1937). William James

Ghent reviews the statistical improbability of financial success for the individual in *Socialism and Success* (New York, 1910). For more genteel criticism see John C. Van Dyke, *The Money God* (New York, 1908); Francis Bellamy, "Successful Men Who Are Not Rich," *Everybody's Magazine,* IX (1903), 604–613; and Brander Matthews, "Standards of Success," *Forum,* XLII (1909), 299–309. The depression of the 1930's revived criticism of the entire self-help tradition. For a typical attack, see Pare Lorentz, "A Young Man Goes to Work," *Scribner's Magazine,* LXXXIX (1931), 205–208.

INDEX